THE WAY *of the* GARDENER

THE WAY *of the* GARDENER

LOST IN THE WEEDS
along the CAMINO DE SANTIAGO

LYNDON PENNER

Printed and bound in Canada at Imprimerie Gauvin. The text of this book is printed on 100% post-consumer recycled paper with earth-friendly vegetable-based inks.

COPY EDITOR: Marionne Cronin PROOFREADER: Alison Jacques
MAP: Kelly Laycock COVER ART: "Botanical background with floral elements in engraved style" by Geraria / Adobe Stock
COVER AND TEXT DESIGN: Duncan Noel Campbell

Library and Archives Canada Cataloguing in Publication

TITLE: The way of the gardener : lost in the weeds along the Camino de Santiago / Lyndon Penner.

OTHER TITLES: Lost in the weeds along the Camino de Santiago

NAMES: Penner, Lyndon, 1980- author.

IDENTIFIERS: Canadiana (print) 20200358685 | Canadiana (ebook) 20200359959 | ISBN 9780889778061 (softcover) | ISBN 9780889777835 (hardcover) | ISBN 9780889778085 (PDF) | ISBN 9780889777811 (EPUB)

SUBJECTS: LCSH: Penner, Lyndon, 1980-—Travel—Camino de Santiago de Compostela. | LCSH:Hiking—Camino de Santiago de Compostela. | LCSH: Plants—Camino de Santiago de Compostela. | LCSH: Christian pilgrims and pilgrimages—Spain—Santiago de Compostela. | LCSH: Gardeners—Travel—Camino de Santiago de Compostela. | LCSH: Gardeners—Canada—Biography. | LCSH: Camino de Santiago de Compostela—Description and travel.

CLASSIFICATION: LCC DP285 .P46 2021 | DDC 914.6/11—dc23

University of Regina Press

University of Regina, Regina, Saskatchewan, Canada, S4S 0A2
TEL: (306) 585-4758 FAX: (306) 585-4699
WEB: www.uofrpress.ca

10 9 8 7 6 5 4 3

We acknowledge the support of the Canada Council for the Arts for our publishing program. We acknowledge the financial support of the Government of Canada. / Nous reconnaissons **l'appui financier du gouvernement du Canada. This publication was made possible with support from Creative Saskatchewan's Book Publishing Production Grant Program.**

Canada Council for the Arts Conseil des arts du Canada
Canada
creative SASKATCHEWAN

For Carol and Dan,
without whom this journey
would not have been possible

CONTENTS

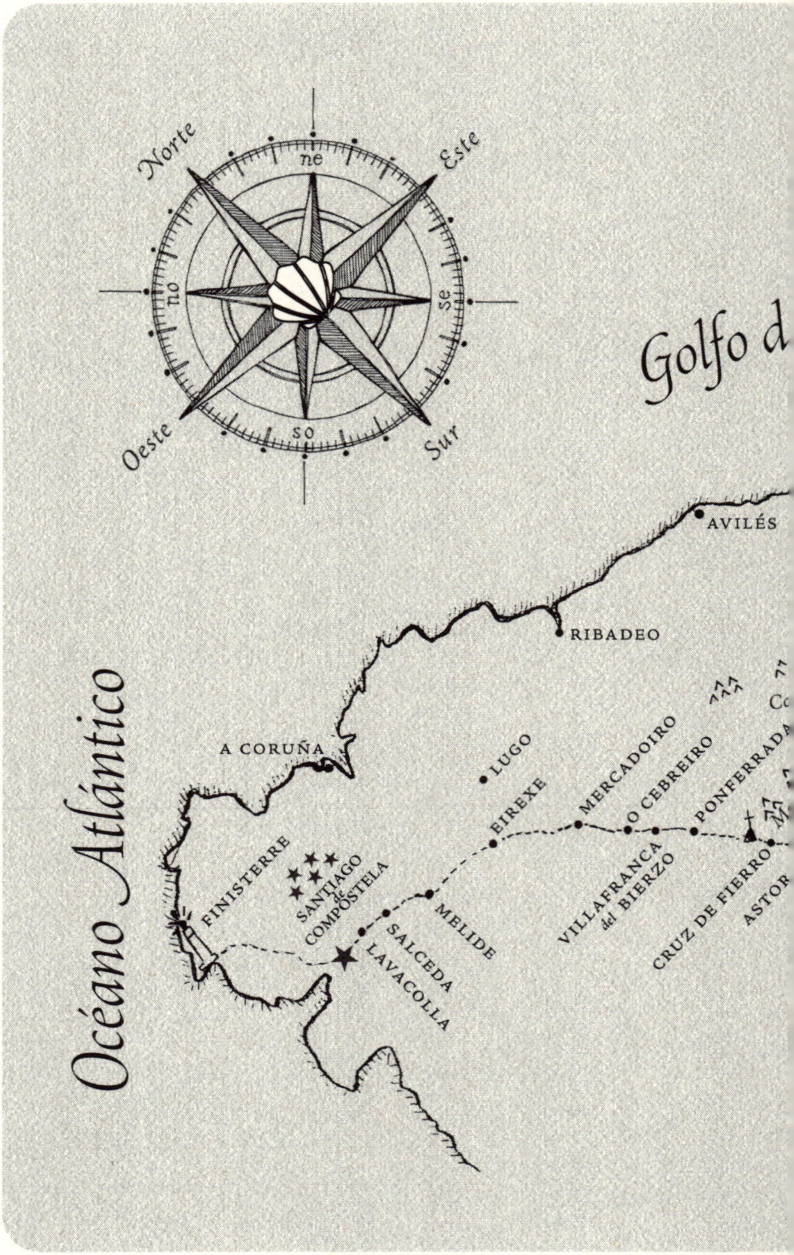
Norte
Este
Oeste
Sur
ne
no
se
so
Golfo d
Océano Atlántico
AVILÉS
RIBADEO
A CORUÑA
LUGO
EIREXE
MERCADOIRO
O CEBREIRO
PONFERRADA
FINISTERRE
SANTIAGO de COMPOSTELA
MELIDE
SALCEDA
LAVACOLLA
VILLAFRANCA del BIERZO
CRUZ DE FIERRO
ASTOR

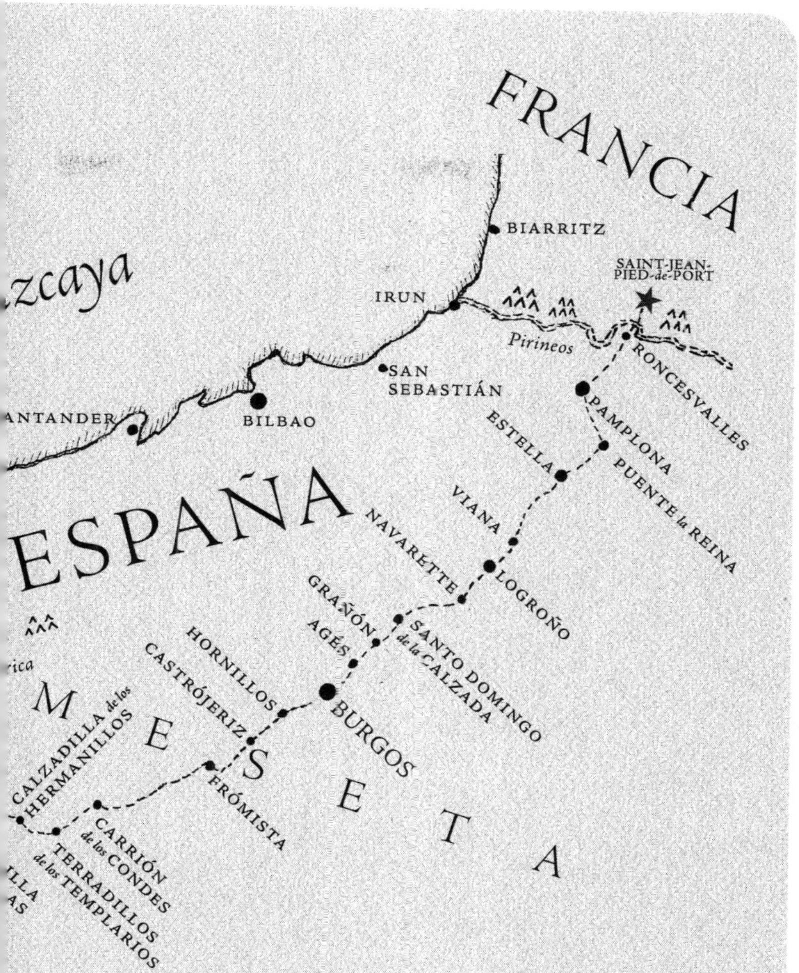
FRANCIA
BIARRITZ
SAINT-JEAN-PIED-de-PORT
IRUN
Pirineos
RONCESVALLES
SAN SEBASTIÁN
BILBAO
PAMPLONA
ESTELLA
PUENTE la REINA
ESPAÑA
VIANA
NAVARETTE
LOGROÑO
GRAÑÓN
AGÉS
SANTO DOMINGO de la CALZADA
HORNILLOS
CASTRÓJERIZ
BURGOS
MESETA
CALZADILLA de los HERMANILLOS
FRÓMISTA
CARRIÓN de los CONDES
TERRADILLOS de los TEMPLARIOS
CAMINO FRANCÉS
772 KM

INTRODUCTION

It started with a beautiful piece of music. I had been invited to have dinner with my friends Dan and Carol at their home in Calgary, Alberta, and the stereo was playing the most exquisite violin concerto I had ever heard. I asked Carol what on earth we were listening to. "This is Oliver Schroer," she said. "It's his *Camino* album." I had never heard of either Oliver Schroer or the Camino. That was how it began.

For over a thousand years, people have been walking the Camino de Santiago (The Way of Saint James) trail across northern Spain. Aside from the journeys taken by the faithful to Jerusalem and Rome, it is the most popular Christian pilgrimage in the world. Each year, hundreds of thousands walk this ancient path to the city called Santiago de Compostela. A beautiful and frequently difficult route, the trail is nearly eight hundred kilometres long and takes many weeks to accomplish, as it is traditionally followed on foot. Ostensibly, the goal is to pray at the tomb of St. James, one of the twelve apostles of Jesus, but, for most, the Camino is far more about the journey than the destination.

Carol had done the Camino a number of years before, but she hadn't been able to quite finish it after she became ill not far from the end. She had decided a second undertaking was necessary, and now that we were talking about the Camino, she asked me if I would be interested in joining her. Not really having a clue what I was saying, I casually replied that of course I would. That was it. Somehow, within a few months plane tickets would be purchased and we would be on our way to Europe.

The great American artist Georgia O'Keefe, whose work I love so much, once said, "I've been absolutely terrified every moment of my life—and I've never let it keep me from doing a single thing I've wanted to do." Airports give me anxiety for no reason at all. Being on a plane or a bus or a train with so many other people is hard for me. I find having to be social *exhausting*. What could possibly be scarier for someone like me than going to a country I've never been to, to a place where I don't speak the language, and immersing myself in an ancient sacred spiritual journey with strangers from all over the world for six weeks? Nothing. Absolutely nothing could be scarier. Nothing could be more challenging or demanding or hard for me. So when Carol asked me to go with her, I *had* to say yes.

I wasn't entirely sure what I had signed on for, but I was optimistic and curious. For most situations in life, a positive attitude and an inquisitive temperament will get you a long way. This is definitely true of the Camino.

I FIRST MET Carol in Waterton Lakes National Park many years ago. She and her husband, Dan, were in one of my wildflower tour groups. I didn't know her, but she knew me. She was an avid CBC radio listener, and for many years I had been doing a garden column for one of the afternoon shows. She knew my voice and my name and introduced herself. I liked her immediately. Carol is in her sixties, but you'd never know it. She has the energy of someone half her age. We became fast friends and remain so to this day. Before the Camino, the only travelling we had done together was to go for a weekend at my friend Shelly's beautiful lodge in northwestern Saskatchewan. Dan is not as strongly inclined towards the outdoors as Carol is, and the idea of walking hundreds of kilometres did not appeal to him, as it doesn't to most sane people. It would just be Carol and me (and several thousand others) making our way across northern Spain.

The route that Carol and I chose to travel was the Camino Francés (the French Way), which is the most popular and the most widely travelled route to get across Spain. There is also a northern route that goes along the coast (it is said to be treacherous), and there is a Camino Portugués (the Portuguese Way), which usually begins in Lisbon and winds its way north.

When we first started talking about walking the Camino, I told Carol I didn't want to go in spring or summer, which is my busy season, when I'm taking care of clients and gardening my little heart out. I thought fall would be better because temperatures would be cooler (Spain is a very hot country) and my calendar would be a little more free and easy. Originally, we had planned to leave in early September, but then my very favourite cousin decided to get married in the middle of September, and I wanted to be home for that. So Carol and I chose September 18 as the day we would leave for our big fancy-pants trip to Europe. We booked our flights in February, and I had the entire spring and summer to prepare.

How does one prepare for the Camino? Well, there are lots of ways, I guess. How does one prepare for any sort of journey? I didn't worry about it too much, but I did spend a fair bit of time researching it and talking to other people who had done the trail before me. I learned more about the treatment of blisters than I ever wanted to know.

The general rule for a backpacking trip is that you do not carry more than 10 percent of your total body weight. I read everything I could find online about what you should pack and what you should not, and I started to get really stressed out about it. Then I decided that I was overcomplicating things and I shouldn't worry; I was doing something that thousands of people have done for hundreds of years. Most of the pilgrims who undertook this journey did not have a Mountain Equipment Co-op nearby or the Patagonia clothing company to order top-of-the-line outdoor wear from. So I decided just to do my best and be practical (I am practical almost to a fault, I have been told) and not stress about it.

By profession, I am a gardener. Unless it's winter, I am usually working outside. My job is very physical. I am always hauling around heavy clay pots and big bales of potting mix and trees and rocks and shrubs and wheelbarrows full of weeds I've just pulled. I also work as a guide in both Waterton Lakes National Park and at the Nikka Yuko Japanese Garden in Lethbridge, Alberta, so I am well accustomed to being on my feet all day. I am not a nine-to-five person who sits in an office chair all week long. And when I have free time, I'm often out . . . on a hike. So I felt well enough prepared just by virtue of the fact that I spend most of my time actively doing active things.

There is a difference, however, between being generally active and going on a hike so lengthy that, day after day, you are walking on average fifteen to twenty kilometres. Carol told me that there may be days when we had to walk twenty-five to thirty kilometres. That's a really long way to walk, and I wanted to be prepared for that. So the first thing I did was buy a really decent pair of hiking shoes. I bought them in March so I could spend the summer breaking them in. You want to be comfortable in them, but you don't want them to be worn out by the time you hit the trail. Don't ask me what brand they were; I couldn't tell you. Brand names mean virtually nothing to me. (For years, I thought Holt Renfrew was a car dealership.) I went to the Outer Limits store in Saskatoon, told them what I was doing, and a nice young man who worked there was generous with his time and knowledge and sent me home with a pair of very comfortable shoes. I paid $250 for them, and to me this seemed an astronomical sum. I had never in my life conceived of paying such an amount for shoes—most of the clothing I own is from thrift stores—but I don't handle pain very well and I had a deep fear of developing blisters along the trail. I wanted to be sure I had taken every precaution to prevent this from happening, and if $250 shoes were the way to do that, then I was on board.

I also decided to start "training," which is sort of hilarious. I don't do marathons. I don't even run. If you see me running it means either I am being chased or I am in pursuit of an ice cream truck. I don't do sports. I find them almost aggressively boring. And I would rather put out a cigarette in my eye than go to a gym and work out. While I'm active, strenuous exercise does not appeal to me in the least. When I say training, I mean I started walking daily. I lost fifteen pounds hauling around a heavy backpack all over the coulees of Lethbridge and the Rocky Mountains for months before departure. I began by doing an hour every day in April and May. In June, I did two hours a day; in July, I did three; and in August and September, I tried to walk four hours a day, but that was difficult to do logistically, so I usually ended up doing two or three. I am fortunate to live in Lethbridge: our beautiful river valley is full of magnificent hills and coulees and provided the perfect challenging terrain to train in.

The other thing I did was buy really fancy, non-chafing underwear that breathes and moves and does all the right things and prevents big, chunky thighs from rubbing together too much, if you happen to have big, chunky thighs like I do. I do not have what is usually considered an "athletic build." I am built for comfort, not speed. A friend once described me as "a decent slab of beef," which I think was intended as a compliment. My point is, at five foot ten and about 225 pounds, I'm pretty average in terms of physical capability, a prairie farm boy who tends to gain weight easily but likes being active.

But I struggled with my weight a lot growing up, and it took me a long time to "own" my body and be even semi-comfortable with it. Even now, I wouldn't dream of wearing a sleeveless shirt or going to a beach. I haven't worn shorts since I was in my twenties. I am super self-conscious about my balding and the fact that my face goes really red if I drink alcohol. I guess there are lots of things we all feel insecure about when it comes to our bodies. The nice thing about the Camino is that no one cares what you look like, or how you're dressed, or your age. One dispenses with vanity very quickly when one has to walk twenty or more kilometres every day.

EVERY PERSON HAS a different lens through which they see the world, and every person expects something different of the Camino. Some people love art and architecture. Others focus on food. Others have a sense of adventure and an urge to explore. Some do the Camino to make new friends and new connections.

I happen to see the world through plants and trees and flowers. I make sense of things around me through gardening and the natural world. Plants tell me about history and climate and soils and people. They speak of times long ago and provide me with clues as to where I am and what sort of things have gone on there. Plants reveal things to me about myself. On the Camino I would keep detailed notes every day of what I was seeing and experiencing, and to my surprise, when I got home and read my journals, I realized just how much of my experience was based on a solid foundation of gardening and plant knowledge. Every step of the way I was observing and interpreting the plants I was seeing.

The Camino is meant to be a spiritual journey, and for me it was certainly that, although not all the time. One doesn't feel "spiritual" every day. And I am not a religious person. I had every opportunity to be one but opted not to choose that path. I grew up in a very Christian household, and by that I mean we went regularly to an evangelical church and to Sunday school. My grandparents often spoke of the Bible, and my mother told my sister and me Bible stories, which I loved. All through my teens and early twenties, I considered myself a Christian. At twenty years old, I was even baptized. Then I began to identify as an atheist, and I have since rejected that as well. I have arrived somewhere in between, in a place of both skepticism and openness, and I think this is a healthy view to have. I am very much open to the idea that there is a God and that God is an active force in the universe. And I can happily accept that I don't know everything. In fact, I know hardly anything. You could fill a warehouse with everything I don't know. I have no idea how it is possible to store nine hundred songs inside my phone, and yet it is a fact. I don't know how a seed germinates, or how lightning works, or how the human eye processes colour. The fact that I lack understanding does not make these things any less real or miraculous. So the conclusion I have come to is that there are forces at work in the universe that are beyond my understanding or comprehension, and that these forces are mysterious, and that's okay.

Over the course of our journey, I would walk through ancient forests of oak and chestnut that were more beautiful than any of the cathedrals meant to house the presence of God. I felt more connected to humanity walking an old dusty trail than I have in any city I have ever been in. But most of the insights the Camino gave me did not arrive until well after I got home. It was a slow-burning candle. I was hungry and tired a lot of the time as I walked. I mostly thought about eating and sleeping, and while I was there I was sure I wasn't thinking many profound thoughts. I was wrong about that. I came home stronger and more self-assured than I have ever been. My tolerance for mediocrity and trivial things has been greatly diminished. My appreciation for the beautiful life I live has increased exponentially. The Camino is a sharp blade; it cuts through to the quick and exposes things, some good and some bad. Who would have expected that a timeworn old path across an ancient land could offer so much?

THE WAY
of the
GARDENER

MONDAY, SEPTEMBER 18–THURSDAY, SEPTEMBER 21

Calgary, Alberta → Bordeaux, France → Saint-Jean-Pied-de-Port

WE LEFT CALGARY ON SEPTEMBER 18, 2017, and spent several days in Bordeaux, as Carol finds long international flights quite arduous. She wanted to be able to relax a little bit and get over jetlag and the time change before setting off on our journey. Being an eager devotee of Julia Child and a lover of French food, I was entirely in favour of this. We stayed in a cute little holiday apartment, and I immediately loved the French people. We didnt cook; we went out and had actual French people cook for us. That was both easier and more exciting. We didn't really "do" a lot in Bordeaux. We walked around the city and went to the magnificent cathedral. We sat outside at outdoor cafés and drank coffee and people-watched. We drank wine in the evening.

One day, we set off to see a small but wonderful little botanic garden (or was it just a well-planted park?) in the city. It was quiet, and according to the Internet, it boasted both swans and squirrels. We saw neither. It was there, however, that I reacquainted myself with the charming little European robin, which I had first met in Scotland a few years before. I absolutely *adore* little birds. What a terrible world it would be without them.

All along the Camino, I would make friends with birds. There were great blue herons and thrushes and wrens and wagtails and even the occasional blue-green flash of a kingfisher over a river. There were great stork nests on nearly every spire of every church (they reminded me of Big Bird's nest from *Sesame Street*). I wouldn't see a lot of wildlife along the Camino, but whenever I did, it made me smile. Lizards would sometimes dart in and out of the grey stone walls, and I would see them basking along shale-covered south-facing slopes. I saw what I thought were large bumblebees, some of which were entirely black with no yellow or orange markings. I later learned they were carpenter bees, which I thought was really cool since we don't have those in Alberta or Saskatchewan. I always said *hola* (Spanish for "hello") to the various farm animals we passed. We share our planet with so many different life forms and other creatures. I feel that they deserve our respect and appreciation, and being aware of their presence made the Camino more fun and interesting.

OF ALL THE different routes one can walk across Europe in order to get to the city of Santiago de Compostela, the most popular is the Camino Francés. It's called the French Camino because it starts in France, but 95 percent of it rolls east to west across northwestern Spain. You start walking in Saint-Jean-Pied-de-Port, in the very south of France, and climb up the Pyrenees mountains on the French side. When you come down on the other side, you're in Spain. Crossing the Pyrenees is widely regarded as the most difficult part of the French Camino, but for me it was also the most beautiful—and my favourite—part.

To get to Saint-Jean, we took the train from Bordeaux to Bayonne, and from there we had to take a bus. I had never been in France before, and I enjoyed the food, the scenery, and the kind and welcoming attitude of the French people. Let me be very clear that I do not speak any language other than English, and I had heard from several people over the years that the French were rude or indifferent to anyone who did not speak their language. I did not find this to be the case at all, quite the opposite in fact. All the French people I met—beginning with the tiny woman named Sophie who drove our taxi from the airport and continuing without exception—were lovely and warm and very accommodating to those who clearly had not taken the time to learn even a few French words and phrases. Saint-Jean-Pied-de-Port is the prettiest, most picturesque little town you could imagine, with cobblestone streets and beautiful stone bridges and great bowers of silver lace vine climbing up the old buildings. When we stepped inside one glorious little antiquated church, it felt like stepping through time. The town is also home to the official pilgrims' reception office, which was the first place I encountered one of the Camino's scallop-shell waymarkers.

No one is sure exactly why the scallop became the official symbol of Saint James (*Santiago* in Spanish). There are many different explanations, depending on who you ask, but Christian tradition holds that James brought the gospel to what is now modern-day Spain. He eventually returned from there to Jerusalem, where Herod Agrippa had him put to death by the sword (see the book of Acts, chapter 12, in the Bible), making him the first apostle to be martyred. One legend recounts that, after his death, James's disciples were bringing his body back to Spain for burial when the ship they were on went down. While nobody died, the body of St. James was lost. The following day, it miraculously appeared on shore, unharmed and covered with scallop shells. There are also other legends that "explain" the association of the scallop shell with St. James.

The origin of the pilgrimage itself is traced to the 800s, when a Spanish hermit is said to have had a vision of a bright star shining down on a particular spot in a forest. According to the legend, an investigation led to the discovery of the burial site of St. James, and the Spanish king, Alfonso II, had a chapel built on the site. The miraculous discovery of the remains of one of the original disciples of Jesus attracted pilgrims from across Europe. It is speculated that the name "Compostela" may originate in the phrase *Campus Stellae*—Field of Stars—referring to the hermit's vision. Eventually, the chapel was replaced in 1211 CE by the magnificent cathedral that stands today and, over eight hundred years later, is still a destination for pilgrims from around the world.

For many devout Christians looking for meaning, the scallop shell has come to symbolize the pilgrimage: the shell's grooves all converge in much the same way that roads from all over Europe converge at a single meeting point: St. James's final resting place in the magnificent cathedral built for him in Santiago de Compostela. The scallop shell is a fitting marker for the Camino and it appears on buildings, sidewalks, and small stone or concrete pillars that indicate the path, marking the "way" for those walking the Camino. But the shell is another kind of marker as well: pilgrims have traditionally carried the shell or the image of the shell to mark *themselves*, so that those they encountered on their journey would be able to identify them *as* pilgrims.

And there is a second, more recent, but also famous, Camino waymarker: the yellow arrow. A priest from the Galician village of O Cebreiro by the name of Don Elías Valiña Sampedro (1929–1989) had studied the Camino in depth and had written a great deal about it. Convinced of its importance, in the early 1980s he started making a serious effort to clean up and mark the trails along the Camino. Starting in Roncesvalles, the first stop on the Spanish side, he painted brilliant yellow arrows to indicate the correct path through the trickiest parts of the way: crossroads and city intersections and places where the trail went into the woods. He packed his car with as much yellow paint as he could and began his trek across the entire northern part of Spain, painting arrows wherever possible to indicate the right way to go. Yellow arrows appear on buildings, sidewalks, fences, and trees to indicate which way one should follow. I blessed this priest often on my journey, as have thousands of other pilgrims, I am sure. If you are in doubt, if you get lost, you can always look for a scallop shell or a yellow arrow, and frequently you find both. Many pilgrims wear bracelets or necklaces with a yellow arrow, and the traditional scallop shells are often affixed to backpacks and coats. For the rest of my life, I will probably look without thinking for a yellow arrow or a scallop shell when I lose my way.

Friday, September 22
Saint-Jean-Pied-de-Port → Orisson

OUR FIRST DAY of walking. Carol and I started out with a beautiful breakfast of croissants, fresh figs, and yogurt at our nice little hotel (*petit déjeuner* might be the only French phrase I learned), and after a quick visit to one of the pilgrim shops so Carol could buy some hiking poles, off we went. The sky was overcast and grey, but no indication of rain appeared, and we began the trek up to the first *refugio* we would stay at: a place called Orisson. It was only eight

kilometres, but it was eight very vertical kilometres. The Pyrenees are relentlessly, deliciously *green*. The sound of cowbells ringing and the bleating of sheep can be heard all along the trail, and it would be hard to imagine a place more tranquil and idyllic. One of the first trees we encountered was a beautiful old English walnut (*Juglans regia*). I would see many of them on the Camino, all the way across northern Spain. As it was almost the beginning of fall, the walnuts were just coming to ripeness, and I gathered some up off the ground. I broke the shells open with a rock, and Carol and I sampled the nuts. They were much better than anything I could buy in a grocery store, still moist and oily inside. It was the first of many foraging activities I would undertake on the path. I put a few in my pocket for a snack later.

That evening, we were treated to a simple but delicious meal of fresh greens, lentil soup, crusty French bread, a lot of wine, and much camaraderie as people from all across the world introduced themselves and we talked about where we had come from and why we were walking the Camino. We met Damian from Australia, Patricia from Italy, Kathy and Rita (sisters) from Canada, and many others. It was a splendid evening . . . until bedtime. The night we spent in Orisson was one of my worst nights on the Camino. Crammed into a small room with a dozen strangers and sleeping in bunk beds is typical of a lot of hostel experiences—certainly nothing I hadn't done before—but I was ridiculously, outrageously *cold*. I literally shivered the whole night and could hardly wait for morning to come. To make things even more interesting, a tiny Korean girl about the size of a button was snoring at decibels that seemed deeply incongruent with her stature. Around six in the morning, I had finally had enough and decided to get dressed and try to find some coffee.

I stepped out into the fresh air and moist darkness of a high mountain night and was engulfed in the most brilliantly shimmering blanket of stars that I had ever seen. Immediately, the full name of the pilgrimage route, the Camino de Santiago de Compostela—"The Way of St. James in the Field of Stars"—became very real for me. I stood there in the cold and darkness, marvelling at where I was. Coffee eventually arrived, and we began our second day.

Saturday, September 23
Orisson → Roncesvalles

YOU WOULD THINK that, living in Lethbridge and working in Waterton, I would be accustomed to wind. I grew up in Saskatchewan, and what constitutes an average windy day on the prairie would be unprecedented in many other parts of the world. But crossing the Pyrenees was *windy*! I am sure the hike was twice the amount of work just because the wind was so fierce and so relentless. Since the Pyrenees form the divide between France and Spain, I assumed that at some point there would be a border sign or a marked boundary or something that told us exactly where we were passing into Spain. No sign ever appeared. When we were not far from Roncesvalles, we encountered a woman selling fresh watermelon to weary travellers from a sort of mobile stand. We asked where we were, and she assured us that we had crossed the border. We had somehow missed seeing it. I heard later it's just a little knee-high pillar and is easy to pass by without noticing. The woman was also very clear that, yes, this was technically Spain, but this was *Basque country* and the people here were *Basque*, not Spanish! Her English was reasonably good, and it seemed very important to her that she convey this to us.

Up over the fields of green we went, looking down upon the most brilliantly emerald-coloured slopes dotted with cattle and sheep. It reminded me of the South Island of New Zealand. Clouds would billow over, obscuring one view before revealing another. It felt transcendent and ethereal, a kind of a liminal region between fantasy and reality. Cows and horses sometimes wandered over the path right in front of us, and goats and sheep could often be heard without being seen. Always, there was the gentle ringing of the cowbells.

In the azure sky above us, great dark birds swirled and circled like immense black snowflakes. I learned later they were griffon vultures and that Spain is home to the largest colonies of this bird in all of Europe. The vultures appeared again and again on the Camino, and it was always thrilling to see them, even though I never got to look at them up close. Vultures have the unenviable yet very necessary task in nature of cleaning up the carcasses of the dead. They are a vital component in sanitation and disease control, and yet most people find them repulsive and ugly. At home in Lethbridge, we have a resident population of turkey vultures, and I have developed a deep and abiding respect for these much-maligned birds who perform the important task of ministering to the dead.

The vultures wheeling overhead on the Camino reminded me of the American poet Mary Oliver's haunting poem about vultures. She describes them as "looking for death" and concludes with a profound observation about eating the dead in order to sustain life. I wondered if there were dead things in my own life that I should be offering to the metaphorical vultures. Indeed, we all have things in our life that become sick and eventually die. These can be relationships, or career aspirations, or sometimes dreams that we lack the time and energy to pursue. I thought many times on the Camino about things I had left festering in my personal life; things that I hung on to that were perhaps better left behind to be cleansed by the vultures.

When we had crossed over the border into Spain, somebody asked if anyone knew what kind of birds were circling above. I said they were vultures. "Gross," she said. "I thought they were maybe eagles or something, you know, like something *nice*."

VULTURES WERE NOT the only faintly magical things I encountered on our trek across the Pyrenees. I also came across the almost mythical alpine thistle and glittering carpets of fall-blooming crocus. The alpine thistle (*Carlina acaulis*) has been prized by rock gardeners for centuries but rarely performs well outside of its home territory. It can be found in a variety of high mountain ranges in central and southern Europe and forms a tight rosette of spiny foliage. Its flowers are large, relative to the plant size, and are sort of a bronzy colour with a silvery sheen. The flowers, which close in wet weather, appear between August and September, giving way to prominent and showy seed heads. It was these seed heads that I found fluttering above the grasses on the edges of the pastures, and they reminded me just how far from home I really was. I never dreamed I would see alpine thistles in their native habitat. During our first few days in Spain, I saw several wreaths made from these thistles on doors and at the entryways of homes. A few places had beautiful carved images of the flowers in wood or stone. I subsequently learned that the Basque people regard the alpine thistle as a symbol of good fortune and blessing, and they have also used it medicinally.

When we think of crocuses, most of us think of spring. Indeed, the true species of *Crocus* are mostly, but not entirely, spring blooming. Many autumn-flowering species of crocus grow in climates more moderate than ours. Most of them produce foliage in the spring, when sunshine and moisture are abundant, then quickly go dormant, and flowers emerge from the bare ground in autumn, courtesy of nutrients stored in the bulb. It is a slightly peculiar thing to come upon small companies of these lilac or purple goblets in a pasture on a sunny autumn day. The blooms open wide in bright sunshine and quickly close again when clouds roll in. The last bees of the year drink deeply from

these little flowers, and the crocuses often grow in great numbers where conditions suit them. All through the Pyrenees, autumn crocuses danced at my feet. I found them utterly charming, and since they are not something I can really grow at home, I thought they were all the more delightful. I sometimes saw them on the edges of the woods too, pushing up through fallen oak leaves and acorns to offer passersby a last little taste of summer.

Sunday, September 24
Roncesvalles → Zubiri

THE FIRST PLACE we stopped once we entered Spain was a former monastery in Roncesvalles, a name that means "valley of thorns" in Spanish. Our evening there was fairly uneventful, except that we were served the most revolting meal on the entire Camino. At 6:00 p.m., we found a small restaurant that caters to pilgrims where, we were informed by some fellow pilgrims, the food was quite good. We stood in line as we were told to do and were seated at a circular table with a number of strangers, whereupon we all began introducing ourselves. We were served stale bread and wine (the wine was okay) and given the choice of either the chicken or the fish. I chose the chicken. Carol chose the fish. We were then served small bowls of a very thin soup that was both cold and unpleasant. We ate it anyway, because we were hungry and surely the rest would be better.

My serving of chicken was small, rubbery, and totally devoid of any kind of spice or flavour; the highest praise I could offer was that at least it was cooked. It was served with soggy, thin fries that tasted like a dirt floor. Carol's fish, which may have once been a trout, was served whole: fins, tail, head, and all. Some restaurants can make this look quite classy, but that wasn't the case here. The fish smelled as if it had been dead and unrefrigerated for three or four days before being cooked. Carol poked it. Its one eye stared up at her balefully and the gaping mouth was locked into a permanent O. We exchanged a silent moment of recognition, and Carol said, "I should have ordered the chicken."

Around the table, others were finding their food similar. I looked at Carol studying her fish. "It's . . . *looking* at you," I said, with a mix of horror and morbid fascination. She tried her very best before finally saying, "I can't eat this." She tried some of my chicken and declared it "unpalatable." We ate the soggy fries. I prayed the rest of the food on the Camino would be better.

WE SET OUT in the dark the following morning. Historically, Roncesvalles and the surrounding woods were said to have been filled with witchcraft. As the sun began to come up I saw, over and over again, trees and shrubs that were traditionally associated with the dark arts. Ash, yew, hawthorn, oak, hazelnut—all of them have been widely regarded as having magical powers for incantations and spells. I wondered if there was any truth to what we had been told about "devilry" being practised in that region. I noticed a great many wild roses too, now heavy with their bright ruby-coloured hips, and realized that it was not for nothing that Roncesvalles was granted its name.

Our destination that day was a little town called Zubiri. It's a pretty place, quaint and old-fashioned, that sits upon the banks of a picturesque river, and there is a beautiful stone bridge and large trees. I liked Zubiri right away, and when Carol and I went out for dinner, we had what was probably the best caramel flan I have eaten in my life. Zubiri was full of flowers—oleanders, marigolds, lobelias, petunias, geraniums, and many others—grown all around the town and frequently en masse, and the whole town was bright and happy and welcoming. It's for this reason it was surprising that our night in Zubiri might have been the weirdest on the whole trip.

People who walk a pilgrimage are usually referred to simply as pilgrims, *peregrinos* in Spanish. They stay in refuges called *albergues*, which are basically hostels that cater specifically to this endless flow of seekers and walkers. These are inexpensive and range from acceptable to quite nice and occasionally extraordinary. Our albergue in Zubiri was clean and comfortable and more than adequate. Our room was filled with a series of bunk beds, and these were occupied by Carol and myself, a woman from Edmonton, two Italian men, an Australian pastor named Michael, and a group of French women with very large suitcases. (I discovered there was a service where, for only a few euros, you could have your bags sent ahead to wherever you were planning to stay that night.)

Off our nice little room were two bathrooms, one clearly marked for men and the other for women. They had sliding doors equipped with locks (not always the case in albergues) and they were easily accessible. As soon as the lights were out for the night, the strangeness began. The French women (I think there were perhaps six of them) were up and down more than a toilet seat at a house party. The whole night, the light in the bathroom went on and off, illuminating the room we were sleeping in and plunging it into darkness again every time. Then there were loud whispers in French. We were trying to sleep, and this began to be very distracting. What were they *doing?* Carol and I later discussed the odd goings-on. We never did figure it out. The light went on and off all night long, but it seemed that none of them actually used the bathroom. At one point, I am sure one of the women inadvertently climbed into the wrong bed, as there was a lot of fierce whispering and someone moved in a hurry.

In the midst of these French women moving in and out like apparitions, Michael, the Australian pastor, decided that he was hungry. He sat up in bed, reached into what was evidently the loudest and crinkliest plastic bag ever made, and began eating peanuts. In addition to the never-ending parade of French women moving around, everyone in the room could hear *crinkle, crinkle, crinkle,* followed by *chomp, chomp, chomp. Crinkle, crinkle, crinkle . . . chomp, chomp, chomp.*

I wish I could tell you that the weirdness ended there, but it didn't. Most of the albergues want everyone to be out and gone by 8:00 a.m. We often left much earlier than this, for two reasons: (1) it helped us avoid walking during the hottest part of the afternoon; and (2) at most of the albergues you can't book a bed in advance, so if you dally too long there might not be anything available for you when you arrive at your next stop. Carol's alarm for the two of us went off at 6:00 a.m. At 6:15, one French woman's alarm went off. In the time we were getting ready, it went off *ten times,* and each time she simply shut it off and went back to sleep. I already mentioned that these women were travelling with exorbitantly large suitcases (instead of big backpacks, like we were), so we can only assume the Camino was a bit of a novelty for them, perhaps to be hiked for a day or two but not pursued as a serious journey.

By 6:30, when Carol and I still appeared to be the only ones awake, I just needed to step into the bathroom with my headlamp on to put my contact lenses in and brush my teeth. The door to the men's bathroom was closed, but it was unlocked and the light was off. Naturally, I assumed it was safe to enter. I slid the door open, and there in the beam of my headlamp sat one of the French women on the toilet. She was naked from the waist down, as one generally is when sitting on the john, with her lacy panties around her ankles. She said "meh" and waved her hand at me in a dismissive fashion. I stood there, frozen. "*Meh!*" she said again, this time with a more vigorous motion of her hand. I closed the door. *Why is she in the men's bathroom?* my brain wanted to know. *Why is she sitting in the dark with the door unlocked?* was my next question.

I went upstairs to the kitchen and told Carol, who was sitting down to a breakfast of very large (and bland) toast, and she was so amused by this story that she laughed until she was nearly in tears—never mind that I was traumatized and still didn't have my contact lenses in. I eventually made my way back downstairs, where the French women and everyone else were now awake. I put my contacts in, brushed my teeth, and we left. Jokes about French women in their underwear followed me around for the rest of the Camino.

Monday, September 25
Zubiri → Pamplona

FROM ZUBIRI, THE Camino takes you to the first major city of the trip: Pamplona. Before you get there, however, the trail leads you on a gorgeous hike over rivers and through woods, across fields and into beautiful little towns full of flowers. I assume this part of Spain gets at least some cold in the winter months, and possibly snow, because I saw a great many plants that require a dormant period. These included lilacs and peonies, but there were also lots of fairly tender plants such as agaves and oleanders. Every little town had lush, well-cared-for vegetable gardens and fruit trees, too. Sometimes these were in small communal lots at the edge of town, and sometimes they were fenced inside little courtyards in front of or beside the home. Streets were shaded by great European ash trees starting to turn gold for the autumn, and nearly every balcony and doorway was filled with containers planted with ivy geraniums and roses, hostas and impatiens. It was nice to see such familiar bright and cheery plants so obviously loved and cherished. Gardens were riots of colour with fig trees and four o'clocks and squashes and grapes. Horse chestnuts and pines provided shade, and angel's trumpet (*Datura*) started to show up on the edges of gardens and fields as a weed. I would see a lot of it before finishing the Camino, often with flowers still open in the early light of dawn. And two blue-flowered plants became ubiquitous. One of these was chicory; the other was pincushion flower.

Pincushion flower is also known by its Latin name, *Scabiosa*. This is a reference to its former medicinal use in treating scabies, but it isn't exactly a pretty or marketable name. Pincushion flower sounds much nicer and is also quite appropriate. 'Butterfly Blue' is a British selection that was honoured as the 2000 Perennial of the Year, and the form I saw growing all along the ditches in Spain is quite like it, only less refined and certainly not as profuse a bloomer. I saw this plant almost daily, in some places still blooming abundantly, even beside the highway, in other places well past its prime. It became a beautiful splash of colour on almost every day of walking.

Chicory (*Cichorium intybus*) is native to Europe but is now widely naturalized in China, North America, and Australia. There are ten species in this genus, but only this one and Belgian endive (*C. endivia*) are cultivated. Growing two to five feet tall, chicory is a large tap-rooted perennial that is occasionally known as blue dandelion. The flowers are indeed a gorgeous shade of blue or pale purple, but on rare occasions they can also be white or pink. It has been extensively cultivated as food for centuries, despite (or perhaps because of) its strongly bitter taste. High in vitamins A, B, C, and K, chicory leaves are used in salads and as a vegetable, and the root is often roasted and ground to be used as a coffee substitute. The blossoms are sometimes candied. Flowers appear from June through September, and the seeds have been added to love potions. Although chicory is highly adaptable, it grows best in a sunny site

with fertile soil. It can become weedy but is occasionally grown as an ornamental in gardens.

In nearly every ditch and along every roadside in Spain, I saw this blue-flowered member of the daisy family opening its showy blooms. It cheered me on days when I thought I couldn't walk any farther, and it appeared in dry places with poor soil that seemed unlikely habitat for any flowering plant. I thought about the deep taproot drawing sustenance from so far down in the ground, water and nutrients that were beyond the reach of fussier, more high-maintenance plants. Plants that have the ability to become weeds often do so because they are so superbly adapted to dealing with difficult situations. Some plants endure difficult growing conditions and some—like the chicory—thrive in them. I suppose that some of us are lucky enough to be like the chicory, too, with deep roots that anchor us and keep us sustained in times of hardship.

PAMPLONA IS POSSIBLY the most famous Spanish city on the Camino. The running of the bulls is not only one of the most celebrated events in Spain, it has become well known throughout the world. The event takes place over a few crazy days in July, but for most of the year Pamplona is a quiet and peaceful city, with big trees, wide squares, lots of pigeons, and a great deal of history for those interested in seeking it out. Its two universities draw students from across the country.

Carol and I had made friends with Sandy, the nice woman from Edmonton who had stayed at the same albergue as us in Zubiri. She ended up walking with us for several weeks, and in Pamplona the three of us shared accommodation in a nice little apartment hotel in the old part of the city and went out in the evening to find a much better meal than the one we'd had in Roncesvalles.

Ordering food in Spain was sometimes a frustrating ordeal. In the first place, the Spanish do not like to eat supper until quite late. Sitting down to the evening meal at 9:00 or

10:00 p.m. is fairly normal. Many restaurants do not even begin serving food until 7:30 or 8:00 p.m. If you have just walked twenty kilometres, you mostly want food and sleep. I was finding walking every day to be invigorating and very enjoyable. While my feet were definitely tired at the end of the day, they were neither sore nor uncomfortable, and when we stopped to rest, I usually took off my socks and shoes for a few minutes to give my feet some air. That seemed to help. But once we'd arrived at our destination each day and dropped our things in our rooms, I wanted to eat. Finding out that food would not be served until the hour I most wanted to be in bed was not ideal, but it often happened that way. We usually went to bed around 8:30 or 9:00, and finding a place that would serve supper at 6:00 or 6:30 could be a challenge.

Then there was the fact that none of us spoke any Spanish. Deciphering a menu could be something of a challenge. A lot of places offer a "pilgrim's menu," which made life way easier. These ranged from not particularly good to delicious to totally outstanding, and even if you knew roughly what you'd be getting, you never knew what form it would take. Ordering pork meant you might get a tiny little circle of meat that was paper-thin and salted to within an inch of its life—or you might get a piece of the most delicious pork you had ever eaten that was big enough to feed three people. If you ordered the fish, you might get a trout with head, tail, and fins attached, or you might get a tiny battered fish stick out of a freezer bag. It was impossible to know what might be coming out of the kitchen, but if you didn't allow yourself to have any real expectations, you were never disappointed—and sometimes you were delighted beyond reason. Pamplona, I am pleased to say, went well beyond our expectations.

Tuesday, September 26
Pamplona → Obanos

THE ROUTE FROM Pamplona to the next stop was not only peaceful and agreeable, it was full of plants and trees I'd been aware of but was not exactly familiar with on an intimate level. The first of these that bears mentioning should really be the figs. If you have never eaten a fresh, sun-warmed fig right off the tree, then you have never really sampled a fig at all. Don't let the squashed, dry, cardboard-textured pressed figs of grocery stores fool you. A fresh and perfectly ripe fig is an object of intense pleasure and deliciousness and should not be passed up.

Figs warrant a closer look because they are truly extraordinary. The genus *Ficus* contains nearly nine hundred species, many of them highly prized for food, medicine, timber, shade, and of course their beauty. They are pollinated primarily by wasps, but not the kinds of hornets or paper wasps that show up and ruin a picnic or swarm your hummingbird feeder. Fig wasps are very tiny, fly-like creatures, and most species of fig have a unique wasp species that pollinates them exclusively.

When you eat the fruit of a fig, you are really eating the blossom. The fruit is actually an arrangement of minuscule flowers held on an inverted, nearly closed receptacle. Botanically, this structure is known as a syconium. Imagine a flower that has essentially turned itself inside out and is fertilized from within rather than from without. One of the Chinese names for figs translates as "fruit without flower," and in other cultures they have been called the trees with invisible blossoms. No other plant does this in quite the same way as the fig.

The syconium is usually bulbous with just a tiny opening at the end that allows the pollinator to enter. The female fig wasp enters this opening seeking a suitable place to lay her eggs and inadvertently pollinates the tree. The flower of the fig itself provides a perfectly safe, comfortable spot for the wasp to start her family. In exchange, the wasp ensures the next generation of figs. No wasp means no seeds. Depending on the species, fig trees can be monoecious (possessing both male and female flowers), dioecious (male and female flowers produced on separate plants), or gynodioecious (producing some male flowers, some female, and some that have both male and female parts). It starts to become very complicated, and botanists have devoted entire careers to studying how figs go about their lives.

The common edible fig (*Ficus carica*) has been grown for thousands of years. In female fig trees, the male flower parts do not develop and instead produce the figs we eat. We do not generally find fig wasps in the female syconiums because the female flower is the wrong shape (too long) for her to lay her eggs in. Miraculously, the wasp pollinates the flower with pollen from the fruit it grew up in! When an edible fig ripens, another fig must be ready to be pollinated. In temperate climes, wasps hibernate in figs, and there are distinct crops. Common figs can have two or three crops per year. The first crop produces small fruits called olynths. Some varieties of common figs do not require pollination at all and will produce a crop of figs (which are sterile) even without fig wasps.

Depending on the species, each fruit can contain hundreds or even thousands of seeds. Edible figs can be propagated by seed or vegetatively, by cuttings, air layering, or grafting. Popular cultivars like 'Peter's Honey' or 'Brown Turkey' have to be propagated vegetatively as they do not produce viable seeds.

While I find the botany of the fig fascinating, it is for more carnal reasons that the fig has so often been revered throughout history. For centuries, the fig has been a symbol

of sexual desire, with some scholars going so far as to suggest that it was the forbidden fruit in the Garden of Eden. Why the association with the flesh? If you slice open a ripe fig, you will perhaps see it. The moist purple-pink insides are often compared to the intimate organs of a woman in a state of arousal. One of the ancient names for the fig is *pagh*, which can also mean vulva. The Latin word for fig, *fica*, can mean either a fig or a woman. Even in the Bible, figs are mentioned in the often very sensual Song of Solomon.

Edible figs require a bit of a chill in the winter, but it must not be not too severe. (There is a reason you don't see fig trees growing on the Canadian prairies.) They survive the winter well enough in places like Vancouver, but they aren't always able to produce a good crop of fruit there. Spain and other Mediterranean countries have an almost perfect climate for these delectable fruits, and they've become an important part of the cuisine and culture.

All along the Camino, fig trees presented themselves. A distinctive and handsome tree, they have lobed, rough-textured foliage and can grow as tall as thirty feet, but are often about half that size. They tend to be multitrunked rather than single-trunked and can live for as long as two hundred years. Some species can live to be over a thousand years old. The prophets of the Old Testament spoke of every man under his own vine and fig tree, and it became a metaphor for prosperity. I can well understand that, as there is something about standing beneath a fig tree and eating its decadent fruit that makes one feel "prosperous." Knowing your grandchildren and great-grandchildren would one day be eating from the same tree must have been a great comfort.

I happened to be walking the Camino at exactly the right time of year for the fruit to be ripe. There, figs are abundant; they grow in cities and gardens, in little country towns, and along abandoned roadways. Some of them were positioned in such fitting places along the trail that I am sure some kind and generous person planted them there deliberately to feed and shade passing pilgrims. I foraged fresh figs on many occasions, often more than once in a day. Sometimes, no one had bothered to pick the fruit and it had fallen on the ground, left to rot and attract flies and hornets. Abandoned fig trees on forgotten farms or in little towns were not at all unusual. I was as ethical and responsible with my "foraging" as I could be: I never picked fruit from people's gardens, and I never opened gates or crossed fences. But if a branch of ripe figs stuck out over the side-walk, it was fair game. Fallen fruit on the ground that hadn't yet spoiled was also mine for the taking. On many days, I would be tired and dusty and weary, only to come upon a beautiful and robust fig offering me her explosive little dusky purple fruits and at once my sprits would lift. Some figs were better than others, but none were unpleasant.

One day I was helping myself to a cluster of figs when a Bible story from my childhood popped into my head. In the story from Matthew, chapter 21, Jesus is on his way back to the city and realizes he is hungry. Seeing a fig tree by the road, he walks up to it but finds nothing on it except leaves. Speaking to the tree, he says, "May you never bear fruit again!" Immediately, the tree withers. His amazed disciples ask, "How did the fig tree wither so quickly?" and Jesus replies, "Truly I tell you, if you have faith and do not doubt, not only can you do what was done to the fig tree but also you can say to this mountain, 'Go, throw yourself into the sea,' and it will be done. If you believe, you will receive whatever you ask for in prayer." When I mentioned this story to a Catholic woman I was walking with, she insisted to me that Jesus would not have done something like that. Cursing a tree, she said, "just wasn't in his nature."

Walking the Camino, I gained more appreciation for Bible stories than I'd ever had before. Jesus and his disciples walked from town to town; they were in a different place every night, and they walked in all weather and situations. Tired and hungry and dusty, they undoubtedly also foraged from whatever fruit trees were available along the road. I found it a bit surreal to be enacting a scene from the New Testament as I made my way to the tomb of St. James. Appropriate, but also surreal.

OFTEN, AS I walked, I thought about how thousands of feet had for centuries trod the path before me. Mine were not the first and they would not be the last. The Camino has changed over the years in the sense that what motivates pilgrims today is likely not what has motivated the pilgrims of the past. I thought a lot about *why* people wanted to walk the Camino so long ago. Why did they persevere? Why did they press on, day after day, far from home, walking much further distances than I chose to?

I think it was a real need. We need our lives to be meaningful; that part hasn't changed. We all seem to want something more. We all want to know that our lives are significant and that we have a purpose. There was a time when people were desperate for hope, desperate for positive change and something more in their lives. Christianity offered that for many, and I think it still does. The idea that you could be physically near to someone, or to the bones of someone, who actually knew Christ, in person, in the flesh, was, I think, a powerful form of motivation and validation that to some extent soothed this need. It made their faith tangible. It was an anchor for their hope and prayers. We want our spiritual experiences to be *real,* and there was virtue in suffering, some reward in putting aside self and pursuing a goal that was difficult and challenging and culminated in being able to pray in the presence of a saint. Santiago was the real thing: the remains of a true saint are said to be housed there.

Walking to Santiago was a legitimate endeavour the faithful could undertake to prove the sincerity of their faith. Sometimes criminals were made to walk the Camino as a form of penance. Wealthy people sometimes paid poor people to make the journey and pray to St. James on their behalf. Walking the Camino gave meaning and purpose to the pilgrims, and there was the added benefit that Spain

was pretty safe. Walking to Jerusalem or Rome, you could be waylaid by thieves or marauders, and those journeys were over land that was more treacherous. Santiago, by comparison, was a relatively easy destination and one that still proved your commitment to Christ.

IN ADDITION TO figs, another appealing tree I was able to reacquaint myself with on the journey was the almond. The difference between wild almonds, dependent on the sky for water, and almonds that are irrigated is like night and day. Spain was in the midst of its most significant drought in forty years, and while fruit was abundant on the wild almond trees, it was dry and tasteless compared to the fruit from trees that were getting a regular watering.

As we walked from Pamplona, at the edge of one town Carol and I came upon a home with a huge almond tree whose branches reached out well beyond the property. I asked Carol if she had ever eaten a fresh almond right off the tree. She hadn't, and neither had I. Almonds are closely related to peaches and cherries. The fruit they produce is a large husk, inside which is a nut, and inside the nut is the seed. The seed is the part that we eat. I picked two of them, and using a stone I cracked them open, offering one to Carol before eating one myself. The explosion of flavour in my mouth was unexpected. It was like opening a bottle of almond extract. I had never been able to reconcile the flavour of roasted almonds with the extravagant sweetness of almond extract. How could they be from the same plant? In that moment, I knew. It was one of the most delicious things we ate on the entire Camino.

ONE OF THE most famous stops on the Camino comes just shortly after leaving Pamplona, at a place called Alto del Perdón, translated loosely as the "hill of forgiveness." There is an iconic series of metal sculptures here, dedicated to all those who walk the Camino. The sculptures depict a stream of pilgrims in single file, on foot and on horseback, and are meant to reflect the historical and eternal nature of the walk. The Spanish inscription on it—*Donde se cruza el*

Camino del viento con el de las estrellas—means "Where the path of the wind crosses that of the stars."

Carol took a picture of me there, and when I look at it I find it hard to believe that I actually went on to walk the entire Camino. The picture proves that I was there, and physically I look capable of covering the whole distance. But I wasn't sure I would be able to. I stressed about getting sick or injuring myself or being abducted or any number of other possible, even unlikely, dangers. Even now, my completion of that long journey still seems surreal and improbable.

BETNWEEN PAMPLONA AND Obanos, we walked through the pretty little town of Puente la Reina. There is a magnificent stone bridge to walk over, with sedums growing in the cracks in the rock. Wild snapdragons (many species of which are native to Spain), elders, and celandine are also common, and it was the only place in Spain that I saw a stork. Usually by late September, they have all migrated south, but I guess this one was taking its time. Stork nests are a frequent enough sight on the spires of churches and other tall structures, and the birds return to them every year. Walnut trees are common in the area (they are common throughout all of Spain), and I noticed that there was a curious abundance of snails. At many places along the road where wild fennel was abundant, we saw great conglomerations of dusty white snails every morning. Sometimes, as they climbed up foliage and stems, they were so abundant they could be mistaken for bubbles or seedpods.

I also saw a scrambling plant that I am sure is a member of the melon family, but I was never able to determine what it was, even though I came upon it frequently. It's okay to not know the name of everything; it is good to be reminded that one has more to learn. I understand, however, the desire to know and to name all the plants one sees. Joseph Banks, one of the founders of the Royal Horticultural Society, was afflicted with this desire, as was that greatest namer of names, Carolus Linnaeus. Naming is a way of making sense of the world. It is a way of organizing things so that the mind can process them. It is also perhaps a means of control, a way of not being overwhelmed by all the diversity and variety one sees every day. There is also a deep satisfaction in learning the name of a plant that has previously been unknown to you.

The walk to Obanos was glorious in terms of plant life. The olive trees were stunning, and great bowers of silver lace vine crept over the old buildings. *Calystegia,* with its white trumpet flowers, rambled through the ditches, and laurels, four o'clocks, lavender, and red salvias filled the gardens. Four o'clocks, prevalent all along the Camino in a dazzling array of colours, grew both in gardens and in abandoned places where they had naturalized. Yews, cypress, crepe myrtles, and camellias offered shade and shelter for passersby as well as birds. European wall lizards played in the rocks. A particular kind of oak (I wasn't sure what) also began to dominate the landscape, and hellebores grew in their shade. Along the edges of the road, Cupid's dart and teasel offered seed heads to the wind and frost. Everywhere I looked, the world was beautiful and full of life. It was late September and the Spanish countryside was showing almost no signs that autumn was on its way, beyond some of the fall-blooming crocus starting to flower, a different species than I had seen in the Pyrenees.

Obanos was the first place I heard digitized church bells. Carol and I noticed that bells were ringing, and upon looking up at the church tower where the sound was coming from, we saw that the bells were not actually moving.

A loudspeaker directly below them was the source of the sound. The world is definitely changing.

Wednesday, September 27
Obanos → Estella

FROM OBANOS, WE set out for Estella, and once again the day's entire walk was just *full* of flowers. *Echium vulgare*, a member of the borage family, was one of the most prevalent plants, much loved as bee forage, but also a serious weed in some parts of the world. I assume it is a native species in Spain, but I might be wrong. I often saw it, with its small blue or purple flowers, growing in waste places and along the edges of roads. Historically, it was used to treat snake bites. I learned that there are five venomous snakes found in Spain, including at least one viper. I actually did see a snake in Estella, what I can only assume was the harmless and fairly common European grass snake.

I saw many common garden flowers growing in the wild along the edges of the Camino path. Musk mallow, malva, spurge, globe thistle, and poppies were quite usual but not always in bloom. Sometimes I was identifying them by their leaves or their seedpods. Crops such as alfalfa and asparagus were easily recognizable, and always there were the olive groves and, increasingly as we went along, vineyards. The great shining fields of grape vines became more and more frequent and were nothing short of enchanting, not least because I do not get to see vineyards at home.

It's always interesting to see familiar trees, such as elms and poplars, growing happily alongside trees that are unfamiliar to you. Southern magnolias are common city trees in Spain, and they must have had a good year, as many of them were abundantly hung with seedpods just starting to burst open. The decorative red seeds were beginning to emerge, and I was asked several times if I knew what they were. Word had spread among the pilgrims that I was the person to talk to if you had any questions about the flora.

I HAVE TALKED about figs and almonds, and the third fruit tree I encountered again and again is no less important. Olive trees (*Olea europaea*) have been grown for thousands of years and are beautiful and extraordinarily long-lived. If there was anything that moved me on this journey, if there was anything deeply mystical and transcendent, more so than any church or cathedral, it was the olive groves. They have the most wonderful gnarled greyish trunks and grey-green foliage that from a distance seems to shimmer. All across Spain, companies of olive trees swayed and glittered in the sun, offering beauty and shade along the path. Some of them were already hung with fruit with the harvest a few weeks off. "I am not in Kansas anymore," I said to myself as I made my way across the country.

I had seen olive groves before, in California, but for me, the olive groves of Spain are something quite different. The way they caught the light was different. The way the leaves rustled in the breeze and the trees hunched over themselves, solid and stocky and confident, was different. Like wine, olives are an acquired taste. I didn't like them when I was growing up, and it was only as an adult that I changed my mind about them. Now, getting to know the olive groves of northern Spain was a lot like getting to know the sibling or cousin of someone who is already a good friend. The olive family (*Oleaceae*) is full of trees and shrubs that I already had affection for. I couldn't live in a world without lilacs. I am fond of the ash. I love jasmine and forsythia. All these are the olive's close relatives, but olives do not grow in my climate. I did not expect on my journey that the fruit of these trees would nourish my body while the trees themselves would nourish my soul.

My fascination with olives started with a tree in our yard, a tree that most prairie people will know as Russian olive. It's a gorgeous tree, but not a member of the olive family at all. It is closely related to some of our own prairie natives such as the buffaloberry and the wolf willow (a shrub whose scent makes many a prairie eye misty and hearts nostalgic), as well as the rugged and stunningly beautiful sea buckthorn. As a teenager, I wanted to find out the difference between the Russian olive in our yard and the olives I saw in the grocery store. I learned that the true olive (*Olea europaea*) is close kin to the lilacs. It is native throughout the Mediterranean and the southern parts of Asia as far east as China. It can also be found in the Canary Islands. While it is now cultivated in many parts of the world, the modern olive has never done better than it has in its native lands, which include Spain. The oil has always been more important than the fruit, but olives provide shade in hot climates, and they offer, more than any other tree I saw on the journey, beauty.

Olives are medium to large trees with elegant leaves that are dark green above and silvery green beneath and orient themselves to face the sun. From a distance, an olive grove can appear to be almost a shade of sage grey or, if it is overcast, as green as any piece of carved jade. Olive trunks are often gnarled and twisted into spectacular shapes. They are an extraordinarily long-lived tree, and many scholars believe that the Garden of Gethsemane, where Jesus prayed on his last night, was not a garden as we understand it but an olive grove. Despite not being religious, I feel I could pray in an olive grove. There is a holiness to olives that can be felt but not easily explained.

Olive flowers are not significant, and if pollinated, they give way to small fruits that at maturity range from green through purple. Most cultivars are self-sterile and require the company of at least one other variety to yield well. In the fossil record, olives go back at least twenty million years, and they have been cultivated for at least seven thousand years. The olive is an old, old crop—so old, in fact, that its ancestry is a bit murky. In many nations, evidence has been found of olive cultivation from well before the time of Christ. Cultivated olives differ from wild olives in that they are far superior. In the book of Romans, the apostle

Paul writes of the gentiles as being wild olives grafted into a cultivated olive: something that simply wasn't done. Grafting remains the preferred means of propagation to this day, and though I looked diligently, I never once saw a wild olive in Spain. I wanted to find one somewhere, maybe quietly flourishing on a hillside minding its own business, soaking up the Spanish sun. I wanted to find an olive that defied cultivation, that had gone out to live life on its own terms. I've read that olives have become major weeds in South Australia, but in Spain they were all on their best behaviour. Each one I saw lived in the company of other olives, gripping the ancient hillsides with their brawny, twisted roots like strong hands.

The Spanish were the first people to bring olive trees to the Americas. In the 1560s, olive seedlings from Spain were planted in Peru. By the 1700s, they had reached California, and now an estimated 865 million olive trees are growing around the globe. They have been a source of wealth for some, beauty and food for others. From the time that Noah's dove returned with a freshly plucked olive branch, to the anointing of altars with olive oil, humans have always known there was something faintly magical about them. The ancient Greeks crowned their athletes with olive leaves and scrubbed their bodies with olive oil. Athena, goddess of wisdom, was credited with giving the olive tree to humankind, and so significant was this gift that the city of Athens was named for her. Some of Jesus's best-known teachings were given on the Mount of Olives. Olives and olive oil are mentioned repeatedly in the Quran; Muhammad called it a blessed tree.

Olives show a remarkable capacity to adapt and flourish on slopes and fields in sunny sites that offer long, hot summers with very mild winters. Any light, average soil will work for them; too rich a diet and they become prone to disease.

Sharp drainage, plenty of heat, and an absence of cold will be declared suitable. They can handle a little bit of frost, but anything below about minus 10 degrees Celsius will harm even a mature tree. They have extensive root systems that allow them to endure drought, and they will remain productive literally for centuries if they are pruned regularly by a competent hand. They grow slowly, and it is for this reason that olive wood is expensive. Wood turners and carvers say it is very fine wood indeed. One can sometimes buy bowls or cheeseboards made from olive wood, and they are strong and beautiful. The bark is thick enough that mature olives have even been known to survive a fire. Spain was in the midst of a major drought when I was there—some said the worst drought in forty years—but I could not tell that from the olives. They were almost glowing with an inner light that suggested to me they keep many secrets to themselves.

Thursday, September 28
Estella → Los Arcos

FROM ESTELLA, WE continued to Los Arcos, another captivating walk, with olives and figs and ash. I saw the seed heads of alliums in the ditch and wondered what species it was. Great curtains of passionflower clambered over fences and the sides of buildings and were hung with bright orange, light bulb–shaped fruits. Superb vegetable gardens full of artichokes and cardoons (they look like silver fountains) and scrubby forested patches of oak made for a day that was sublime and peaceful. I also saw marsh mallow growing in moist places in the ditch and thought how amazing it is that so many people have no idea it is a real plant.

Marsh mallow (*Althaea officinalis*) is not imaginary. Many gardeners happily grow rose mallow, mountain

mallow, and others, but it rarely occurs to people that the confection we call marshmallow must have its origins somewhere. Closely related to hollyhocks, the marsh mallow is a perennial native to Europe, western Asia, and the northern parts of Africa. It has a long history of medicinal use, but it is believed that the ancient Egyptians were the first to cultivate it for food.

Growing anywhere from three to four feet tall, this is not a showy plant. It tends to be quite erect, with thin stems and grey-green foliage. The small flowers are pale pink and resemble musk mallow, usually appearing in August or September. As the name would imply, marsh mallow favours moist to very wet areas, and sometimes even grows in shallow water. The tough, thick roots are ivory on the outside, white and fibrous on the inside.

It was the roots that were prized for both food and medicine. They are mucilaginous and sweet. The ancient Romans valued them as a vegetable. It was often recommended that they be boiled first and then fried with onions and butter, and people today who have cooked them say they are quite tasty. The sticky, sweet consistency of the roots eventually led to them being candied and sometimes preserved in syrup. This became a delicacy in many parts of the ancient world. The modern confection we call marshmallow contains not the remotest trace of this historic plant, which is really disappointing. I wondered how many pilgrims through the centuries knew and recognized this plant and perhaps harvested some for their supper in the evening.

The gap between what was considered common knowledge then and common knowledge now is growing. The number of people who have no idea what food looks like before it arrives on their plate is staggering. I have worked for people who had no idea that some beans are climbers and some are not, and I once had to explain to someone that pumpkins are not harvested from a tree. While we might laugh at this, it illustrates just how far removed we are from things that were once familiar and commonplace, and three hundred years ago many Europeans, I expect, would have known a marsh mallow when they saw one.

Friday, September 29
Los Arcos → Viana

WE HAD BEEN experiencing some particularly hot days, so Carol and I started leaving really early in the morning to avoid having to walk in the most intense heat of the day. I thought doing the Camino in September and October would help us avoid hot weather; I was wrong.

On the way to Los Arcos, I had started getting some pain in the top of my foot and the lower part of my leg. Now, as we headed for Viana, it intensified and became sharper. Little did I know this was the beginning of shin splints, something I had no prior knowledge of. I ignored the pain, not knowing what I had done or what was causing it. I focused instead on a beautiful tall grass with fluffy, bronzy-white plumes that grew in great abundance in many places along the path. I wasn't able to identify it, but if I ever do, I might try growing it here at home. Another frequent plant was a medium-sized, viciously spiny shrub covered in smallish blue fruits. My first thought was that it was a barberry, but closer inspection revealed it to be a species of plum. Commonly called sloe or blackthorn, *Prunus spinosa* is found across Europe and is used in Spain to make a kind of alcohol called *pacharán*. Distractions such as these gave me something other than the incipient pain to think about, and so I just continued on my journey.

In Viana, we again stayed in a pleasant little apartment-type hotel. We had been walking quite a lot with a very nice couple from Melbourne named Mark and Isobel. They were to be staying in the apartment next to ours. We were given a key (do not even get me started on the hopeless situation that is locks and keys in Spain) and told to go up to the third floor. To get there, we had the option of taking the stairs or the elevator. The elevator was approximately the size of the phone booth that Superman used to change clothes. One person could have fit very comfortably in this elevator. Mark and Isobel both got in, and then so did Carol. I said that, obviously, with my giant pack (which by now we had christened "El Grande") there was no room for me and I would take the stairs. "Just get in!" said Mark, and he pulled me inside. I was wrong about there being no room at all left in the elevator; the door shut, and it is no exaggeration to say there was only *exactly* enough room for all of us. I'm quite sure that I've dated people I didn't get this intimate with. All four of us began to laugh hysterically, because the elevator was now (very slowly) going up and it struck me that if this elevator got stuck, it was literally going to be hours before anyone noticed we were missing. If one of us had to pee, it would be the worst situation possible. When the door finally slid open on the third floor, I was sure someone would have to release us with a pry bar. But we were, in fact, able to extract ourselves from the tight quarters. We laughed about that elevator for the rest of the trip.

WHAT WAS EL Grande so full of? It's a good question. I didn't use a camera during this journey, but Carol and Sandy and Isobel certainly did. I have seen some of those photos, and in most of them we all look as if we have been dragged backwards through a hedge for some distance. We are covered in dust and dirt, and Carol insists that her hair looks terribly messy. There is nothing glamorous about the Camino. A sacred journey is not necessarily a journey in which you look your best.

Since you have to carry everything on your back, being selective about what you take along is important. Basically, you need just what you're wearing and one change of clothes. It's amazing how little you need to carry. You'll want a water bottle for sure, and sunscreen, and toothpaste, and all of those sorts of things. You have to bring your passport and your wallet (tuck those in a safe place), and I couldn't have done this journey without a good set of hiking poles.

You need decent hiking socks so that you don't get blisters, and a really decent pair of shoes that are well worn in, but not so worn that they'll fall apart on your walk. A good pair of hiking pants and shorts, a couple of light, breathable shirts, and a jacket and an umbrella. A hat is a good idea too. I wore a bandanna instead, because I'm kind of a badass like that. Oh, and you'll need underwear that won't chafe and bunch and end up stuck between your ass cheeks (a condition known as "hungry bum").

The pack needs to be roomy enough that you have space in there for everything, but not so big and heavy that it's a burden to carry. It's a hard balance to maintain. I had borrowed El Grande from a friend, and I think he was about twenty pounds when packed (El Grande was a "he"). He was very accommodating. I even carried a small jar of peanut butter in there for Carol, who liked to have it with a bit of toast in the morning. I had plenty of room. It wasn't a problem. I didn't mind carrying El Grande, but when I discovered that there was a service where you could have your pack sent ahead and were free to walk without it during the day, I did that fairly frequently. Not every day, but often. It's an act of faith, hoping your pack will actually be at your next stop when you arrive, and luckily for me it always was.

El Grande was full of surprises. I wasn't accustomed to carrying all my worldly goods on my back, and I wasn't super familiar with the pack itself. El Grande had all kinds of hidden compartments and zippers and pockets and clips and strings of some sort. When I was packing for the Camino, I made it a point to have really good hiking underwear, which is expensive, and I packed it away in El Grande and apparently forgot about it. Just before I left, I went through the bag again and thought, *Didn't I pack any underwear?* So I repacked it. The result was that I had thirteen pairs of underwear or something ridiculous like that and didn't know it. Somewhere along the way (I think we were in Pamplona), I noticed a bulge in the bottom of El Grande and began investigating. I found one of those hidden pockets, opened it up, and discovered I had an entire menswear store in there. Extra socks and everything. I told Carol, and she said something like, "A *dozen* pairs? You've been carrying around over a *dozen* pairs of underwear?!" Yeah, I had been.

When you have to carry everything with you all day every day, any extra little bit of weight matters. I decided, with some regret, that I should probably throw out some of my underwear. This was not as easy as it sounds. I think I already said I have big tree-trunk thighs, and I was afraid of not having enough underwear in reserve in the event that my clothing was stolen from a clothesline in an albergue somewhere. This occasionally happens. Mine was *expensive* underwear, and I'm not Rockefeller. Where would I find replacements if I needed them? What if my thighs rubbed together so much that my hiking pants started on fire? (My brain leans toward the dramatic and the improbable.) But the Camino is all about leaving things behind, I guess. I did wonder, though, what the maids cleaning the albergue the next day would think when they found seven pairs of underwear in the bin.

Saturday, September 30
Viana → Navarrete

WE LEFT ONCE more in the early-morning dark, with me trying to ignore the pain in my left leg. On the way to

Navarrete, we walked through half a dozen pretty, quiet little towns—a magnificent church in nearly every one—full of petunias, carnations, and vegetable gardens, with vineyards and olive groves all around them. In one place, I saw a squash vine stretched out luxuriously along a stone wall with its ripening fruits lolling about in the sun.

ALL ACROSS THE Camino, there are depictions of St. James. This makes sense; it *is* the Way of St. James, after all. He's almost always shown as a rather robust figure, typically decorated in some way with a scallop shell and often carrying a staff. On the top of this staff is an unusually shaped gourd. I like gourds, so this made me curious.

Gourds belong in the same family (*Cucurbitaceae*) as squash, pumpkins, melons, zucchini, cucumbers, and luffas. I really, *really* like this family of plants. Pumpkins in particular incite in me a kind of rapturous, profound joy that I cannot explain. They make me gloriously, *exuberantly* happy. I once read an article about "cucurbitaceans," people who are subject to this upwelling of joy from this group of mostly burly and beefy vines. So I'm not the only one who has this condition. The fact that St. James apparently travelled around with a gourd makes me suspect that he was something of a jolly (and practical) fellow who would have been good fun to sit down and have a probably very tiny cup of coffee with. (More on the tiny cups of Spanish coffee in a moment.)

Most of the true gourds are native to Africa and Asia, and they have been known for thousands of years. There are, fittingly, even references to gourds in the Bible. Most gourds are very fast-growing annual vines from the tropics and subtropics, and their cultivation is the same as for pumpkins and squash, though they have a much higher tolerance for humidity. Typically, gourds have small yellow flowers that give way to strange, whimsical fruits that can be warty, winged, ridged, flattened, oblong, pear shaped, spoon shaped, globe shaped, or any combination of these. The fruits can be white, ivory, red, yellow, any shade of green, orange, or buff. Although they are not poisonous, they are generally considered unpalatable and have little, if any, flavour. In many parts of Asia, gourds are eaten as a delicacy, but they are picked when very, very small and often heavily battered or seasoned.

What is interesting about gourds is how they are utilized throughout the world. In Asia, they are best known as food. In Africa, they are items of utility, with all manner of things being made from them, and in North America they are regarded as decorative or ornamental plants. This has led to mass breeding of gourds and a plethora of different varieties to choose from, should you have space enough to grow them in your garden. Most, but not all, gourds belong in the same genus as pumpkins and squash. When you find "ornamental gourds" for sale at the farmers' market or grocery store in the fall, what you are usually looking at is the offspring of *Cucurbita pepo* var. *ovifera*, heavily crossed and backcrossed throughout the years. One of the nice things about gourds, unlike their relatives, is that the vines are usually more than strong enough to support the fruit, and therefore they can be grown on trellises and arbours. Their fast rate of growth and tropical appearance has made them a favourite of many gardeners. Heights of ten to fifteen feet are common. Gourds need heat and abundant water to do well, and they are especially sensitive to a frost.

Most gourds are pollinated by bees, but those with white flowers are often night-blooming, and these are pollinated by moths. When the gourds are ripe, the tendrils nearest the fruit will usually shrivel up. The gourds need to be dried before they can be used for anything, and this can take several months. When fully dry, a gourd should rattle when shaken. These are the seeds inside. After they are dry, they can be coated with lacquer or shellac and used indefinitely. They are ideal for making birdhouses or any number of artful projects such as bowls, dippers, or decorations. In many parts of Africa, gourds are referred to as calabash and are used to make everything from musical instruments to drinking vessels. This was the purpose of St. James's gourd: it served, most likely, as a vessel to drink from. Well-cured gourds are (mostly) waterproof, extremely lightweight, and very durable. They cost practically nothing and would have been the ideal thing for a traveller to reach into a stream to get him or herself a drink of water. Forget the Nalgene bottles of today; if you were a pilgrim centuries ago, you would go about with a gourd. I also suspect that St. James carried a gourd with him just because he liked gourds, as I do. I bet he was secretly a cucurbitacean. What apostle of the Lord would *not* have been delighted by such a plant?

The story of gourds doesn't end there, though. If you've had a bath lately, you might have scrubbed yourself with a luffa (also spelled loofah or luffah). The luffa (*Luffa cylindrica*) is a gourd native to the northern parts of Africa and still much grown in Egypt. It is left on the vine to mature until nothing is left but the xylem membranes inside the fruit. These are like rough, very porous sponges and are often used for exfoliating the skin (though what you buy in the store as luffa these days is almost always synthetic). Luffas can do well in most of Canada, but they need a long season of intense heat and abundant water. The white flowers are large and very pretty. I have tried growing them only once, and I wasn't very successful. I wonder if, in addition to his drinking gourd, St. James carried a luffa to clean himself up in rivers and streams along the way.

WHY AM I so sure that the coffee I'd have with St. James would be served in a tiny cup? That's how the Spanish do it. You basically get a shot glass full of coffee (or half a shot glass) and that's your lot. I started drinking coffee when I was in my early twenties. I quickly realized the difference between good coffee and bad, and I'm just a little bit of a coffee snob. Coffee is one of the reasons I feel motivated to do anything. Sometimes, when I get into bed at night, I get really excited about the coffee I'm going to drink the next day. This probably indicates that I have a problem. I don't care. I love coffee.

Europeans have a different attitude toward coffee than North Americans do. We like very large servings of it, which we often consume on the move, and we will not be held accountable for our actions if we don't get enough. Any accusation of wrongdoing can be sidestepped by saying, "Sorry, I haven't had my coffee yet today." Everyone accepts this explanation. Europeans, on the other hand, believe that coffee should be served in small, dainty cups (thimbles, really; they serve coffee in thimbles) and that for full enjoyment it should be savoured slowly. In theory, I agree with this.

But imagine you have just gotten up and you have to walk at least twenty kilometres today. You have to walk over some formidable terrain. You have to leave early in the morning, when it is still dark and rather cold. Before you leave, you would like to grab some coffee, but all you're allowed is less than a quarter of your usual quantity, and you cannot take it with you; you must sit down and drink it where you are. Granted, it will be delicious coffee. It will be coffee so dark and rich and fragrant you will dream about it for months afterward. It's such a very tiny amount, though, and you're still tired from the big walk you did yesterday. Now, repeat this every day for six weeks.

I began to feel bitter about my inability to purchase a large coffee. I really wanted a very *large* coffee! I realize I am painting a very unflattering picture of myself, but all I was thinking was, *I'm tired, and I have a long way to travel today. Can I please get a very large coffee to go?* The answer, though, is no. You cannot. This is Europe. You will sit down and drink your coffee like a civilized human being, and you will drink your coffee from a tiny vessel as God intended.

On the hotter days, I sometimes craved an iced coffee, and you would think that in a country as hot as Spain, iced coffee might have caught on. Apparently it hasn't. Maybe in summer, but I never saw iced coffee on offer. I drank sangria instead. Once, I borrowed Isabel's iPad to figure out how to ask for an iced coffee in Spanish. I wrote it down very assiduously. I was sure it could be done. In the next *tienda* we visited, I carefully ordered an iced coffee. The woman behind the counter made me my usual tiny cup of coffee, then motioned to me to wait. She went into the back room and returned a moment later. She dropped an ice cube into my hot coffee and went back to scrubbing the bar.

IT WAS AROUND this time that the Camino first began to frustrate me. We were about two hundred kilometres into our eight-hundred-kilometre journey, and I felt like I wasn't making any really good friends. If you read accounts of the Camino, either on the Internet or in the various books people have written about it, what comes up as a recurring theme is that you make friendships that last a lifetime. The people you meet are often cited as one of the reasons to actually *do* the Camino. But I found that the Camino disconnected rather than connected me.

Granted, on most days I'm not especially social. I am self-employed, and I live alone. My communication with others is usually through text or email. I am often working in a garden or in the wilderness somewhere, and much of this activity is solitary. I don't mind this; I enjoy it. In fact, I spent months before I left for Spain mentally preparing myself to spend all day every day with people, and I made a promise to myself that I would be friendly and engaging and make an effort to establish new connections. I was walking with Carol, but we didn't stay together all the time. Sometimes she walked ahead of me; sometimes I walked ahead of her. Sometimes you walk for a little while with people you meet along the trail. Then you stop at the next bar or *tienda* and have a seat and there are . . . people. You sleep in albergues, usually in bunk beds, and you are surrounded by . . . people. You'd think it would be fairly easy to make friends with people if you are surrounded by them every day. For me, that was not so.

I had also decided before leaving that I would leave my cell phone at home. I didn't want to be distracted with business or work, and I really wanted to focus on my journey. I thought it would be a good idea to spend a few weeks not constantly checking my phone. At first, this was definitely positive. Eventually, though, I just started to feel cut off. I'd left my iPod at home too, another thing I shouldn't have done. Music would have been a great help. I was the only person I encountered who had decided to make the trip "technology free."

Upon arriving at the albergue, most people would find a place to sit and rest after showering or doing laundry. Then, everyone would get out their phones and spend the rest of the afternoon uploading pictures to Facebook or Instagram and talking to loved ones back home. People were social, but often they spoke a language I didn't understand. And even if they spoke English, having a conversation over coffee with someone is not the same as getting to know them. It's not that I didn't make any friends on the Camino, and it's not that I didn't meet anyone nice. It's just that I didn't meet anyone with whom I established one of those deep "soul" connections that Oprah likes to talk about. I never met anyone and thought, *Oh, this person* gets *me*. But I suppose I don't often think that about people I meet at home, either.

I've always liked plants and animals more than I like people. I do have some very good friends and family whom I love deeply and go out of my way to spend time with, but I am one of those people who doesn't always play well with others. Like porcupines and great horned owls and black widow spiders, I am mostly solitary. For as long as I can remember, wild places like forests and river valleys and grasslands have held huge appeal for me, while shopping centers and cities and apartment buildings have always made me feel vaguely desolate and unhappy. I suppose I thought that, on the Camino, I was going to suddenly evolve into a much more advanced human. Maybe I thought I would somehow be able to be one with the wilderness and be able to be deeply connected with other humans at the same time. It doesn't usually work that way, I found. I am just never going to wake up one morning and find that I am suddenly the Dalai Lama. To be fair to myself, I did manage to enjoy both the wild places on the Camino and the people I met, so perhaps for a moment in time I actually *did* evolve.

LOGROÑO, ROUGHLY HALFWAY between Viana and Navarrete, is a nice little city that we walked through in the heart of La Rioja's wine-growing country. Trumpet vines, a few with flowers still remaining, and Japanese creepers were busy covering up the sides of buildings, and cedars and silver poplars and willows were abundant.

As it happened, it was here in Logroño that I became acutely aware of the Spanish love of smoking. I am very sensitive to nicotine, and if I am around people who are smoking, I react to it. My eyes start to get red and irritated, my nose starts to run, and I get a very unpleasant prickly sensation at the back of my throat. I am lucky enough to live in North America, where restaurants and flights are non-smoking and most of our workplaces are smoke-free. In Europe, it seems like *everyone* smokes. Cigarettes can still be bought out of vending machines (something North America hasn't seen since the 1980s). I found it vaguely offensive when waiters brought me an ashtray the minute I sat down. Why would they just assume I was a smoker? Every terrace is filled with people smoking, and clouds of cigarette smoke billow down every street and alleyway. There is no such thing as stepping outside for a breath of fresh air at a Spanish coffee shop. Spain has a *farmacia* (indicated with a green cross) on every corner, yet amazingly no one seems to have clued in that smoking is bad for you.

Going into public spaces in Spanish cities was often a real hardship for me. Not only did the smoke make me feel physically ill, it also annoyed me that people were just allowed to light up wherever they wanted. I found myself often not wanting to go out in Spanish cities at all. I'm sure that, because of my insistence that we not sit on patios or terraces, I became an irritant myself to the people I was travelling with. Maybe it's my imagination, but I found European cigarettes to be especially foul, both in France and Spain. If you happen to be a smoker, you will probably love Spanish cities. If you are not, consider this your warning.

ONE OF THE more enjoyable things about Logroño is how nicely planted it is. Oleanders, Queensland palms, lindens,

paulownia, honey locust, and silk trees are all common. Despite the pollution and cigarette smoke, they appear to be in very good health and flourishing.

Of particular interest is the Camino de Santiago rose, developed in Logroño and extensively planted in parks and gardens. It was introduced in 2012. The flowers are an orangey-coral colour with intense pink highlights and a strong fragrance. I found one sign—thoughtfully written in Spanish, English, and French—that explained that the goal of this rose is to offer beauty and encouragement to those walking the Camino. I thought that was rather lovely.

Sunday, October 1
Navarrete → Azofra

MY SHIN SPLINTS had downgraded themselves from extremely painful to mostly just uncomfortable by this point, and by day fourteen, walking all day didn't seem like work; it just felt normal. At the start of the Camino, you're saying stuff like, "Oh my goodness, that's another twenty kilometres from here . . . ," but by the end of it you're saying, "Pffttt . . . that's only another twenty kilometres. Let's do it!"

I continued to make friends with every fabulous plant I encountered. The evening primroses were stunning. Their large, soft flowers—the colour of lemon meringue—were still open when we left at dawn. There was wild rosemary with branches nearly an inch thick. I have thought about paying $6.99 for a few sprigs at Safeway, and here was a rosemary taller than I was, with no one paying any attention to it at all. Four o'clocks and ivy geraniums and petunias showed up in every garden and container, and nobody uses marigolds as exuberantly as the Spanish do. Figs and walnuts and ash and oak leaned over me by the side of every scrubby trail. I discovered the beautiful St. Mary's thistle growing wild along the ditch. I've always rather loved thistles even though I know they are usually weeds. St. Mary's thistle has the most fabulously marbled foliage and is said to be painted that way because the Virgin Mary spilled some of her milk on it while nursing the Christ child. It has been used medicinally for centuries.

I also saw my old friend the charming little European robin (quite different than the North American robin), the hilariously named blue titmouse (close relative of the chickadee), and the very pretty European goldfinch (which also is quite different than our North American species).

IF YOU HAVE spent any time in Europe, you will likely have noticed the age-old practice of pollarding. This is a pruning system in which a tree is severely cut back to stimulate the growth of dense, supple new shoots. It is usually done to trees that grow very large in order to keep them at a much smaller height.

Historically, trees were pollarded in order to produce fodder for livestock, poles for making fencing, or fuel for burning. Willows, hazels, maples, lindens, sycamores, and London plane trees are all street and boulevard species that are regularly pollarded in Europe. The practice began over a thousand years ago, when walled European cities simply did not have room for large trees. (Victor Hugo's famous character Jean Valjean, in *Les Misérables,* is a tree pruner, most likely someone who did pollarding.) I find the practice ugly and unnecessary and always recommend that people plant the right size tree for the right area. If you plant a tree that tries to grow to sixty feet tall and has to be regularly pollarded to keep it at thirty, why wouldn't you just plant one that doesn't exceed thirty feet? That way, you don't have to pay someone to prune it every other year or so and it could retain its natural shape and its dignity. Very soft new growth is also much more prone to disease, and I saw many pollarded sycamores on the Camino that were so white with powdery mildew it appeared that someone had shaken a bag of flour over them. In some places, I even saw trees whose branches had been grafted to those of their neighbours. I'm not sure what the goal of this was, but other pilgrims said the trees appeared to be dancing. My thought was more that they appeared handcuffed to each other: trees forced into captive servitude.

Monday, October 2
Azofra → Grañón

ON THE WAY to Grañón we walked through quite a lot of oak forest. Actually, oak forest was abundant along the entire Camino. I was forever trying to figure out what species of oak I was actually looking at, and of course oaks planted in towns and cities are usually imports from other lands and not the same as the native species. All of the best European fairy tales (Hansel and Gretel, Little Red Riding Hood, Rapunzel, and many more) feature deep, dark forests. I assume this is a reference to oak forests, since their canopies are so dense they block most of the light from reaching the forest floor. To early people, the forests must have seemed very threatening. On one hand, they provided firewood and food, but on the other hand, wild beasts lived in them, and if you believed in magic the woods could be very scary indeed.

Oaks belong in the genus *Quercus*, and there are more than six hundred species known. They are members of the beech family, and as such their closest relatives are the beeches and the chestnuts. They come from all over the northern hemisphere, some deciduous and some evergreen, and from many different kinds of habitat. While most are very large trees, a few of them are shrubby. Many are of horticultural importance; others are highly valued for their timber. Some have been used for food or medicine, and others have had religious significance.

Oaks have distinctive, simple leaves that are often deeply lobed. They generally have wide, spreading canopies and are excellent shade trees. Male and female flowers are produced separately but on the same plant. They are pollinated primarily by the movement of the wind, but insects also play a role, and the seeds are very familiar: we know them as acorns. Oaks are well known for their long lifespans (often several centuries) and their deep, carrot-like taproots. They favour rich, fertile soil, and while many are drought resistant, all are better when water is available. As a general rule, they are rapid-growing when they are young, with growth rates slowing dramatically the bigger they get. They are resentful of disturbance, and if they must be transplanted, this should be done when they are as small as possible. Some oaks produce magnificent autumn colour, others hardly any colour at all, or at least inconsistently. Their wood is strong, heavy, and very dense. They have been prized for thousands of years for building boats, cupboards, cabinets, and strong furniture. The cathedrals of Europe were built primarily from beams of oak, in part because the wood is very strong, but also because it is resistant to both fire and rot.

Despite being very bitter, acorns are highly nutritious and have been used as pig feed for centuries. The great carpets of fallen acorns (and beech nuts) are referred to as "mast," and pigs were often released into the woods in fall to feed on this rich diet. They can eat fifteen to twenty pounds of acorns in a day, and when they are sufficiently fattened they are slaughtered. While walking through a Spanish city one day, I saw a menu posted outside a restaurant that was in both Spanish and English. The English version said something about "ham from acorns." I assumed it was from pigs fed on mast, but Carol suggested that perhaps it was a meat substitute not unlike tofu.

I hope she was joking, because a ham substitute made from acorns would be pretty horrible.

Many oaks live in symbiotic relationships with fungi in their roots, and highly prized truffles often grow beneath oaks. As if that were not enough, oaks are high in tannins and are used for the production of leather and wine barrels. Even the corks we use to plug the wine bottles are derived from a species of oak. The tannins found in the leaves are very resistant to rot and take a long time to break down on the forest floor. The carpet that develops acts as a mulch for woodland perennials, as well as creating habitat for beetles, spiders, centipedes, snails, and many other small creatures.

Acorns, and therefore oak trees, have been recorded as a food source since as early as 4000 BCE. The Roman poet Ovid called them the "first food," dropped from the tree of Jupiter. They were not only nutritious (albeit awful-tasting) but also an easy food to store, and they did not spoil quickly. Acorns were eaten during lean times when better food was unavailable, and the Celts were known to pulverize them into a kind of flour.

There is perhaps no tree in history as revered as the oak. I was not unaware of this as I walked the Camino. They have been cultivated since antiquity and are mentioned in several places in the Bible. Usually the tallest trees in the forest, they are the most likely to be hit by lightning. For this reason, the ancient Greeks associated the oak with Zeus, king of the gods and master of lightning. The Romans called him Jupiter, or Jove, and for both civilizations the oak was a symbol of bravery and strength. Dione, perhaps the most mysterious of all the gods on Olympus, was sometimes called the "Shining One" and was the adopted mother of Aphrodite. Her sacred oracle, near Athens, was an oak grove, and you could make an offering to her and ask a yes or no question. If the leaves rustled, the answer was yes. Silence meant no.

To the ancient Celts, the oak was a symbol of strength and masculinity. The highest caste and most venerated people in Celtic society were the druids, and although the origins of this word are obscure, many scholars believe it comes from the Greek words *drus*, meaning "oak," and *wid*, meaning "knowledge" or "to see." The word essentially means "those with oak knowledge." Oak trees once covered more than 90 percent of the British Isles. Today, only 1 to 3 percent of that original oak forest is estimated to still stand in the United Kingdom. The Celts were people of the woods and great worshippers of nature; they had many sacred oak groves.

The oak was the symbol of Herne, protector of the fields, forests, and woodlands, and nearly as sacred to the Celts as mountain ash (rowan) and yew. The Celts' religious beliefs, like many religions, started with a "mother goddess" concept. The mother goddess was Danu (from which the Danube takes its name), whose name means "water from heaven." Water symbolized the female element and femininity in creation, while the oak symbolized the male and masculinity. The mother goddess, in the form of water, nourished the oak and gave it birth. When Christianity came to Europe, many sacred oaks continued to be worshipped, particularly in France, where we have "Our Lady of the Oak" in Anjou, and there are many places where beautiful old oaks are decorated with pictures of the saints.

To most people walking the Camino, an oak forest is merely a welcome respite from the hot sun and a peaceful, pretty place to walk. For me, the oak forests were much more than that: beautiful, yes, but also a living testament to history and times long past. One's appreciation and enjoyment of them is much deeper when you know the span and breadth of their history and cultural significance.

WHEN WE WALKED from Azofra to Grañón, we had to pass through the little town of Santo Domingo de la Calzada. The founder of the town, St. Domingo, built a bridge, a hospital, and a hotel to accommodate those who were walking the Camino, but the town is also famous for another reason: as I recorded in my journal, it is home to "the church of the chickens."

St. Domingo was a former hermit who decided to dedicate his life to ministering to the needs of pilgrims walking the Camino. He also began building a church, which became the cathedral of St. Domingo. While Catholic churches in Europe can sometimes be a bit austere, the cathedral of St. Domingo is different. In beautiful bas reliefs and sculptural details in the stonework one can see images of many farm animals, not least of which are the chickens. The saint's tomb, located right in the church, is directly across the way from a high, gilded cage in which a rooster and a nice little hen seem to be happily going about their lives.

This is to honour the miracle of the chickens that allegedly took place here in the middle of the fourteenth century. Legend holds that a virtuous and very godly family—mother, father, and teenage son—stopped to rest for a few days on their way to Santiago. While they were in Santo Domingo, the innkeeper's daughter became deeply infatuated with the son. She made her feelings known to the boy, who, being on a holy pilgrimage, declined her advances. Enraged at being rejected, the girl took the family silverware and hid it in the boy's pack. After the family was well down the road, she reported the "theft" to her father.

Understandably upset, the innkeeper had the local constabularies pursue the family, and when they were apprehended the items were indeed found to be with the boy. He pleaded his innocence, but the local magistrate did not believe him, and because he was now thought to have stolen *and* lied, he was sentenced to death by hanging. His parents were overcome with grief, and as a final cruelty the judge said that after the boy was dead he was to be left hanging for a week as a warning to any other would-be thieves.

The boy was hanged, and despite their immense sorrow, the parents felt they had no choice but to complete their pilgrimage. At dawn, they returned to say a final goodbye to their son before going on their way. When they got there, they found the boy hanging but fully alive and calm. He told his parents in a gentle voice that they should not be afraid, because "blessed St. Domingo" was holding him in his arms. "Run and tell the magistrate," he urged them, "and St. Domingo will provide another miracle."

Astonished and full of joy, his parents ran to the home of the magistrate, who was just sitting down to breakfast. The magistrate was most unhappy about being disturbed first thing in the morning, but the couple was very insistent. After listening to their tale, he assured them that they were terribly mistaken; their son could not possibly be alive. "He is no more alive," said the magistrate, "than these two chickens here on my plate." (I would like to know who eats two chickens for breakfast, especially in Spain.) It was then that St. Domingo performed his second miracle, because at once the roasted chickens grew feathers and beaks and began clucking and crowing, miraculously restored to life. The magistrate fell to his knees in fearful penitence and began to beg the Lord for forgiveness. Then he rushed with the parents to cut down the boy, and one assumes they all journeyed to Santiago together and lived happily ever after. There is no word regarding what became of the innkeeper's daughter.

The two chickens that came back to life were taken to live out the rest of their (newly restored) days in the church, and it is said that the two chickens kept there today are their direct descendants. They are maintained by the priests and must never be eaten. It is also said that if you happen to find a feather from one of these chickens (they sometimes make it to the cathedral floor), it is a guarantee that your pilgrimage will be successful. And if the rooster crows while you are in the church, it is said that you have found special favour in the eyes of the saint. I found no feathers and did not hear the rooster, but it's the only church I've ever been in that had sacred poultry.

Tuesday, October 3
Grañón → Villambistia

THE PATH FROM Grañón to Villambistia took us through pleasant forest glades (where signs indicated in Spanish that European badgers live there), through open, scrubby areas where angel's trumpet (*Datura*) had made a weed of itself, and into a sunny, open site where a jumping spider landed on me and said *Buenos días* before wandering off to find a fly or some other suitable prey.

Carol and I had accumulated a small group of fellow walkers around us by this point. There was Sandy from Edmonton, Scott from Florida, Mark and Isobel (with whom we had shared the world's smallest elevator), and Glenn and Sue, a couple from Austin, Texas. As we walked past hydrangeas and vineyards, roses and sunflowers, fields of cauliflower and calendulas growing by the wayside, we all got to know each other. We also started to see ripening quinces (*membrillo* to the Spanish) on the trees, which was something I'd not seen before. We saw enormous stork nests, prominent on the spires of nearly every little country church, and when we stopped walking each day, we fell into the pleasant habit of drinking sangrias. The sangrias I drank in Spain were the best I ever had.

OVER THE COURSE of the Camino we walked beside, and through, so many vineyards. White grapes and red grapes and table grapes and grapes of all kinds and shapes and descriptions. Few plants have been more important to mankind than the grape vine. We have cultivated them for thousands of years. It is not an exaggeration to say that I found our passage through the vineyards rather mind-blowing. I had only ever seen vineyards in British Columbia and California, and often not at the time of year when they really looked like anything. I didn't pay much attention to them. But that late summer and early fall as I walked the Camino trail, the vineyards appeared again and again and again.

I found myself considering, over and over, the meaning of the grapes. Grapes have been on our planet for a long time; fossils found in India have placed them as far back as sixty million years ago. All grapes belong in the genus *Vitis*, and there are nearly eighty accepted species. They comprise their own family (*Vitaceae*) and are closely related to Virginia creeper (*Parthenocissus spp.*), which covers so many barns and Quonsets across the prairies. Most are from the northern hemisphere. The flowers are insignificant but give way to clusters of the familiar berries that we call grapes.

I never knew much about how to grow grapes because I don't live in a climate that is particularly hospitable for them. While there are now some extremely hardy and very reliable grape cultivars one can grow in zones 2 and 3 (such as 'Beta' and 'Valiant'), they weren't so common when I was first really getting into gardening. These hardy forms actually carry genes from the river grape (*Vitis riparia*), which is mostly native to the eastern half of North America. It ranges into Manitoba and can even be found, rarely, in the extreme southeastern corner of Saskatchewan. The idea that any kind of grape could be native to my home province I find rather astonishing.

The river grape is widely regarded as the hardiest species of grape in the world, and it has been much used in breeding programs to develop hardier, better quality cultivars and selections that can withstand harsh growing conditions. It grows in coulees, in ravines, and near creeks, generally places with fertile (but not overly rich) soil, moisture, good drainage, and full sun. It scrambles through and over any shrub in its path and eventually grows up to ten feet tall. The vines are very handsome, occasionally developing good fall colour, and become very woody with age. The berry-sized fruit is very small and black, with a distinct blue blush to the skin. These grapes have a flavour and texture similar to 'Concord' grapes but are more tart. They can be eaten fresh (they are sweeter following a frost) but also make excellent wines and jellies. Over seventy-five different species of animal have been documented eating the fruit, and some years the crop is especially abundant.

Upon seeing the highly cultivated, deftly managed descendants of wild grapes flourishing on sunny south-facing hillsides in Europe, I wasn't sure what to think. I couldn't help but compare the lavishly tended modern grape to the wild river grape that climbs up through the wilds of eastern Canada. I decided that some people are probably cultivated grapes, and some of us are river grapes. I am a river grape, no question.

Over and over again, we saw vineyards in varying stages of harvest. Some had already been picked clean; others were merely ripening. Some were just starting to lose their leaves; others had been severely pruned in order to become more fruitful in the next year of their lives. As a river grape, I reflected on how hard life must be for a cultivated grape vine, clipped this way and that, harshly pruned and never allowed, for its own good, to do quite what it wants. There's a lesson in that somewhere. Left to their own devices, hybrid grapes could become unfruitful or diseased or sick.

The wine grape (*Vitis vinifera*) is believed to have originated in Southern Europe and the southwestern parts of Asia. It is something of a chameleon, as plants with a naturally wide distribution often are. Some forms produce smaller leaves than others; some grow very tall, while others don't; some produce particularly good fruit and others do not; some have more tolerance for frost than others; some are vigorous, and others, sluggish. From this great diversity, vine keepers have bred innumerable different grapes. About 70 percent of the world's grape harvest is used for wine, and wine is everywhere in Spain. It isn't even really considered a luxury; it just miraculously appears on your table when you go to eat somewhere.

I did not grow up in a household where wine consumption was usual. In fact, to the best of my knowledge, my parents still don't like wine very much. We have the occasional glass at Christmas time, but it was never part of our daily meals or evening rituals. I was a teenager when I first tasted wine, and I couldn't believe that people drank that stuff. It tasted awful.

Wine is an acquired taste, and if you don't grow up with it in your house, you will always feel just a bit rebellious and a little bit sinful when you drink it. I remember in Sunday school having to memorize a verse from Proverbs that says, "Do not gaze at wine when it is red, when it sparkles in the cup, when it goes down smoothly." Wine leads to drunkenness, and drunkenness is a sin, we were told. I remember being slightly scandalized the first time I went to a party as a teenager and someone asked if I would like a glass of wine. I most certainly would not! My grandmother had two brothers who became alcoholics, and she has told me on more than one occasion that this would never have happened if they would never have had that first drink. I became somewhat concerned that if I indulged in wine, I would soon be a raging addict and it would ruin my life forever. Wine was none of my business, I decided.

Imagine my surprise when I actually started to *like* wine. I will never be a wine enthusiast, but I do like a glass now and again. I drank more wine in my six weeks in Spain than I probably did in my entire life prior to that, and it's not that all we did was drink. If I wasn't having a sangria after the day's walk, it was a glass or two of wine. Sometimes it was red, sometimes white, depending on which region of the country we were in. Some of it was very good, some of it was only acceptable, but I don't really remember ever having a "bad" glass anywhere.

BY NOW, THE Camino was beginning to develop its own particular kind of rhythm. Every night, we went to bed in a new place; every morning, we got up and walked. Every day, we examined where we were and what we were doing and thought about all we were seeing. Several times on the trail, early in the morning, I would see little mice returning home after a night of foraging. Hawks often sailed overhead. I loved those hawks. I knew they were different from the hawks I enjoy here at home, but I considered them friends. A hawk is something familiar and powerful and comforting when you have grown up in a place where they are abundant: so alert, so aware of their surroundings, and always watching everything that goes on. I liked knowing that someone was watching over me on the Camino. A hawk observing my movements was as comforting as any unseen angel might have been.

I have always been deeply fond of birds of prey. Whether they are hawks or owls or falcons or even herons, birds that kill and eat other species really interest me for some reason. Spain has many different birds of prey, not just hawks. At one little town, an interpretive sign on the trail pointed out some of the common birds of prey that one might see. The sign was mostly in Spanish, but the pictures were good, and I was pretty delighted.

I've already spoken of the griffon vultures. The other raptors we saw soaring high above us were usually kites. I presume they were the red kite and the black kite. There are a number of kites native to North America, but none to be found where I live. Kites are larger than hawks but smaller than eagles, generally, and they frequently have forked tails. They tend to favour open country and feed on small animals such as rats and mice. They typically have a weaker bill and less capable talons than their relatives, as well as distinctly long, rather pointy wings.

Spain's national bird is a bird of prey. The Spanish imperial eagle (*Aquila adalberti*) is considered a threatened species and is found only in Spain and Portugal. It is a magnificent and very large bird that feeds mostly on rabbits but actually isn't all that fussy. Loss of habitat and illegal poisoning seem to be the main threats to the survival of this species. They were seriously endangered by the 1960s but appear to be rebounding in number thanks to conservation efforts. However, I certainly didn't see one during my time in Spain.

I have also always really liked magpies and was astonished to see one from the window of the cab when we left the airport in Bordeaux. I had sort of forgotten there were magpies in Europe. Most people who grow up on the prairies do not like them. This is because they tend to be very noisy at 5:00 a.m. And it's true that they will actively seek out the nests of songbirds in order to eat the eggs or unfledged young and will sometimes take delight in tormenting cats or dogs. But there are lots of things to like about magpies. For one thing, they're beautiful. On first glance, they appear black and white, but if you observe them closely, you'll see alluring shades of iridescent dark green, especially in their tail feathers. Magpies are something gorgeous that I see almost every day, a reminder to look for beauty in the world. Sometimes I really need that.

Magpies are also highly adaptable and extraordinarily clever. They are believed to be among the most intelligent of all birds (second only to ravens and parrots) and, unlike most others, can recognize individual humans. And if you pick on one magpie, you're picking on every magpie in the neighbourhood: all his buddies will come to his aid. They really have each others' backs! Magpies are also good parents and devote a lot of their time to building huge, elaborate nests of twigs and sticks. These are so well constructed that hawks, owls, and crows will often appropriate magpie nests to use as their own.

I also greatly admire their adaptability. At one time, magpies mostly followed wolf packs and cougars and other predators around, picking up their scraps and scavenging. The arrival of humans meant terrible things for a lot of animals because they just couldn't adapt to what humans were doing to the landscape. Magpies flourished. How many other species have significantly benefited from humans? Depressingly few. Magpies have flourished in our towns and cities, using the trees we plant for nesting sites and raiding our garbage and recycling bins. They patrol Tim Hortons parking lots looking for scraps (much like their forefathers did with predators) and they not only survive but flourish.

If you have picked up or held a magpie, you know that they weigh practically nothing. Their entire body is mostly feathers and beak, and when I see magpies flying in our formidable prairie gales, I am always so impressed. It must be so much work for a bird that weighs the same as an envelope to fight and fly against such wind. I love them so much I have a prominent magpie tattoo on my right arm. I feel like I am a bit of a magpie myself. I am sometimes overly chatty (especially if I'm nervous), I like to get up early in the morning, and I will go out of my way to protect my family. For me, the magpie is a symbol of endurance and strategy.

When I discovered the Eurasian magpie in Spain, I was thrilled. Overjoyed, actually. It is a different species than what we have here at home and is certainly not as common; I didn't see one every day, but I did see them reasonably often. Every time I saw a magpie, it was like a visit from a friend. I usually pointed them out to Carol ("Look! A magpie!"), which was met with polite indifference. My lovely companion Carol can't stand them. I felt much the same way when she said, "Oh, look at this beautiful church!" Each to her own.

AS THE DAYS went by, I realized I was finding things to laugh about with the others and be amused by, and I started to feel a lot less alone. Everywhere we went, petunias and ivy geraniums practically poured out of the sides of old stone buildings. Who knew that such ordinary and common flowers would be so loved here? Nearly every small home had at least a few flowers, often ordinary and unassuming, but sometimes I saw unusual things, such as snow on the mountain (*Euphorbia marginata*) or mimulus or *Impatiens balfourii*. Yuccas and roses are common garden plants in northern Spain and both easily recognizable. Many of the towns had extensive plantings of locust (*Robinia*) that were just starting to develop their vivid yellow fall colour, and I

thought about how spectacular it must be in early summer when they are in flower and how good they must smell. I bet bees come from all over Spain to drink their nectar.

Wednesday, October 4
Villambistia → Agés

VERY OFTEN ON the Camino you walk beside or through great looming forests where the trees stand tall and appear to look down over you. Seeing Scotch pine in the wild was really cool. It's a common enough tree for shelter belts and parks in Canada, but seeing a tree in the wild is always really special. It's like visiting a friend at their home instead of at work.

But we also saw many forests that clearly had been planted, presumably for the production of timber. These trees were in extraordinarily straight rows, a precision that suggests it is to facilitate harvesting. You can always tell when a forest has grown there by itself and when it has been planted by humans. Sometimes the trees themselves were a clue. I often saw both Douglas firs and eucalyptus (neither of which is native to Spain) growing as though they belonged there, but the arrangement and the fact they were non-native clearly indicated that someone had planted them. For me, there was something strangely unnatural and at the same time natural about these artificial arrangements.

Another common sight all along the Camino is the blackberry. There are at least half a dozen species of blackberry in the world and many hybrids, so I don't know if the ones I saw in Spain are naturally occurring or if they were introduced from elsewhere. Commonly referred to simply as "brambles," the thorny plant could be found almost everywhere we walked. Often they were scrambling through trees and shrubbery with their heavily armed stems right at eye level. It's amazing I didn't meet anyone who had injured themselves on one of them. There is something to be said for the plain tenacity of the blackberry. It seems to thrive in almost any site and is hell-bent on dominating the landscape. In many places, it was evident where it had been severely hacked back and warned sternly, "This far you may come and no farther."

The Camino frequently offers small jewels, unexpected moments as bright and encouraging as any flower. Once, a grasshopper with shining blue wings leapt up in front of me. Another time, a butterfly that looked curiously like our own native tiger swallowtail went fluttering past. Early in the morning, there were often little colonies of bats zipping about beneath the street lights.

Thursday, October 5
Agés → Burgos

ON THE FAIR and radiant morning that we walked from Agés to Burgos, we walked underneath half a dozen horse chestnuts, one of the most popular street trees in Europe, and as I was admiring their shiny, large, brown-red seeds all over the ground, we passed by a home where several pots of red carnations were in flower. I knew they were significant, but it took me a moment to remember why: the red carnation is the national flower of Spain. At the time that I was walking the Camino, the province of Catalonia had decided to declare independence, which was all the talk in every newspaper and constantly on TV (televisions were often on with a live newsfeed in the coffee shops we stopped in). Many people opposed to the revolution put up pictures of red carnations, as a call for unity I suppose. Carnations are a simple, well-known, and uncomplicated flower, and I will never be able to see them quite the same way again. For the rest of my life, they will make me think of Spain.

Friday, October 6
Rest Day, Burgos

THE CITY OF Burgos is one of the largest on the Camino, with a population of just under two hundred thousand, and we decided it was a good place to take a rest day. Burgos is famous for its many ancient churches and convents and also for its cathedral. Carol, who had previously been to the city, was very excited to see the magnificent cathedral once more. Churches and cathedrals are not a huge draw for me, but I appreciate beautiful architecture as much as anyone, and when was I going to be here again? We decided to take our time in Burgos and see some sights. The cathedral was pretty much the main item of interest.

What can be said about Burgos Cathedral? Construction began in the year 1221, and the building has all the attractions that cathedrals usually have: magnificent stonework and brickwork, towering spires, depictions of the saints, history, grandeur, and an awe-inspiring marriage of beauty and functionality. I'm not any kind of expert on buildings, but those in the know about these things say that Burgos Cathedral is extraordinary. It is a UNESCO World Heritage site, and thousands of tourists come from all over the world to see this great structure, which has stood so solidly for so long.

Carol had spoken highly of the cathedral, and I was actually very excited to see it. We got ourselves there, stood in line, paid our entrance fee, and in we went. It was surprisingly dark inside, and also very quiet. It is not an exaggeration to say that Burgos Cathedral is *magnificent*. This is a word that gets thrown around very casually, but in this case it accurately describes the place. As with many of the great churches and cathedrals of Europe, the interior was completely over the top. You are literally surrounded by some of the best stonework ever produced. The piers, the vaulting, the soaring height . . . all so deceptively simple looking and yet so complicated at the same time. The enormous altarpiece was *dripping*—almost literally—with gold. The cathedral is dedicated to the Virgin Mary, and the great depictions of her and the other saints were enormous and overwhelming. I could not turn in any direction without seeing gold. The altars, the statues, the saints in the ceiling, gold seemed to flow over it all like water. It took about ten minutes for me to go completely around the cathedral. I started to feel unwell.

I couldn't stop thinking about an event I had gone to in Calgary a few years before. The Mexican performance artist Astrid Hadad had put on an incredible show in an arts festival there. She told the story of Mexico's history through song and dance and outrageous costumes. During the show she also spoke, through a translator, to provide absolute clarity about the meaning of each performance. She recalled a trip she had taken to Spain and how all the churches and cathedrals she had seen there were covered in Mexican and South American gold. She said, "The gold on Spanish altars was purchased with Mexican blood." This struck me so forcibly I have never forgotten it, and it came back to me vividly in that moment.

The air around me began to feel oppressive, like a heavy weight. I tried to think about something else, but I couldn't get the words of Astrid Hadad out of my head. My throat seemed to be narrowing and it was getting harder to breathe. I told myself I was being ridiculous, and again I tried to focus on the beauty and craftsmanship I saw all around me. I walked around the cathedral a second time, but all I could feel was darkness. Not physical darkness, but a kind of emotional and spiritual darkness. I had never felt like that inside a church before. It was like all the weight and significance of history was bearing down upon me. All I could see was lust and greed for gold. I sat down in one of the pews and tried to manage my breathing, but everywhere I looked, every angle of the building, made me feel oppressed and sickened. The images of saints became ghastly apparitions. Their faces started to look demonic. The stone walls made me feel like I was trapped in a tomb. The shining gold was dirty and shameful.

I couldn't take it anymore. I fled from the cathedral. Outside, in the sunshine, I sucked in great lungfuls of air and tried to compose myself. I was able to find a little park where a few London plane trees were growing, and I put my arms around their trunks and looked up at the sky until I felt okay. It took at least fifteen minutes for me to pull myself together. I have never, before or since, felt so strongly oppressed or horrified in a place of worship. Churches usually make me feel peaceful, if they make me feel anything at all. Later, when Carol and others were talking about how profoundly beautiful Burgos Cathedral was, I remained quiet and said nothing. Later, I privately told Carol how I felt about it, and I think she was very surprised. No one was more surprised than me, I have to say.

Saturday, October 7–Monday, October 9
Burgos → Hornillos → Castrojeríz → Frómista

AFTER OUR TIME in Burgos, we were ready to hit the road again and tackle one of the most famous, and sometimes dreaded, sections of the Camino: the meseta.

Some people love the meseta, and some people hate it. Depending on how fast you go, it occupies anywhere from seven to ten days, and you're walking on rough Roman roads that are terribly hard on your feet. If you're going to get a blister on the Camino, it will be here. (My shoes and socks held up beautifully on this trip, but on the meseta I put Vaseline on my feet every morning to reduce the friction and help to avoid blistering. It works very well, I might add.) I suppose if I had spent my life in a downtown skyscraper in a city, I might find the meseta overwhelming or perhaps difficult to process. The people who write of the great open skies, the great freedom, and the fresh air and beauty of the meseta, I suspect, are city people. It reminds me very much of the stretch of the Trans-Canada Highway that runs from Swift Current to Medicine Hat. That part of the highway has a lot of big open skies, farms, and rolling grassland on either side. It takes about two and a half hours to drive that distance, and I always like it. If I had to walk it, though, I think I would find it very tiresome, as it would take many days. Three days of walking the meseta was fine; after that, it quickly became very monotonous and I just wanted to be done with it and walk somewhere pretty again. If you are thinking about walking the Camino, the meseta is not a section you need to do if you're a farm kid from Saskatchewan. It won't be anything you've never seen before. Consider taking the bus from Burgos to León.

The first day we walked the meseta was dry and windy, and by the end of it we were covered in dust. A Frenchman who had done the Camino several times told me that the first part of the journey was very physical, the second part was very mental, and the third part was very spiritual. I kept hoping for profound spiritual thoughts on the meseta, but I never really had any. I thought about food mostly, and my nephews.

WHEN THINGS START to stress me out, or I begin to despair, I think about my nephews. While I walked the meseta, my thoughts often lingered over them.

I am never going to have children. This is not a lament, simply a statement of fact. I can't remember a point in my life when I wanted to be a father, and I used to actively dislike children. I always anticipated that someday my sisters would have kids, but I was indifferent to this fact. It just felt inevitable and had nothing to do with me. I didn't know how important my nephews would become for me until well after they were born. I'm not sure exactly when I started to see them differently, but somewhere along the way my nephews started to endear themselves to me. It is not an exaggeration to say that I stopped disliking children because of them. They have made me more patient, more understanding, and more open-minded.

I went through a particularly dark time a few years ago, and one of the things I held on to in that horrid place was the thought that if something happened to me, it might hurt my nephews. If you are prone to falling into mental darkness at times, as I am, it helps to have something to ground you and keep you real. My nephews have done that for me. I recognize more and more how important they are to me, and my sisters have told me that I am important to my nephews as well. I am sometimes surprised at the ferocity with which I love those boys, and I cannot imagine what it would be like to love a child that was my own. I think it would be too much for me.

Somewhere along the Camino, I overheard someone say, "every footstep is a prayer." I think I rolled my eyes; it was early on, and people tend to be overly spiritual right off the hop. But as I strolled across the dusty meseta, I found some truth in the notion. Every footstep was perhaps not a prayer exactly, but it certainly brought awareness. I was aware of the ground beneath my feet; I was aware of my body and the weight of my pack; and I was aware that I was on a journey in a foreign land. Perhaps this sounds trite, but all those yoga instructors who told me to "be in the moment" and "really be present" suddenly sounded very logical and reasonable. I alternated between being very alert to my surroundings and letting my thoughts drift. Who, I wondered, would my nephews be when they were adults? What role would I play in their lives? Who would they love? Would they become parents themselves? Would they grow up to be religious, and would they ever be inspired by the fact that Uncle Lyndon once walked eight hundred kilometres across Spain for no apparent reason?

I sometimes consider that perhaps my Camino journey had absolutely nothing to do with me and is meant to play some role in my nephews' lives many years from now. Perhaps, when faced with a crisis, one of the boys will consider the examples and influences in his life and say, "Uncle Lyndon went on a great pilgrimage and he's one of my favourite people; perhaps I will do the same thing," and this might lead him down a path to something he needs. Perhaps, while I was out here, dusty and tired, with great big semi trucks flying by (a good portion of the Camino is beside a highway), it wasn't about me but about the example I was setting.

Sometime after we returned home, Carol commented that the Camino was like "a really long walking meditation." I thought that was quite accurate.

Tuesday, October 10–Wednesday, October 11
Frómista → Carrión de los Condes → Terradillos de los Templarios

BY OCTOBER 10, still on the meseta, I was really exhausted, not so much from walking but from being with people. Mark and Isobel, Glenn and Sue, and Sandy had, along with Carol, become my regular crew, and that was great, but

I was starting to feel like I needed some alone time. This can be in incredibly short supply on the Camino. There were several days where I just had to make it a point to be alone inside my head, and like anything else in life, if you practise this you get good at it.

Walking from Frómista to Carrión de los Condes was as pretty as the meseta gets. We were making our way along an ancient Roman canal system. It was surrounded by willows and alders and poplars, all common-enough trees that I knew from home. Agrimony and wild rosemary also grew in abundance, and when we finally got into town, there were once again flowers in planters nearly everywhere. I saw geraniums and roses and sweet williams and lavender. I spotted a man driving with a large pot of aloe in the passenger seat beside him, and it made me smile because that was totally something I would do. I wondered if he was a gardener.

The Spanish grow beautiful vegetable gardens, and while I often saw leeks in their well-kept plots of land, I rarely, if ever, saw leeks mentioned on any menu when we were in a restaurant. I saw a poinsettia in one window and wondered if they are as popular a houseplant at Christmas here as they are at home. I was still having some pain in my shins and left foot, but I was also still ignoring it. We had a beautiful dinner when we finally got to town, one of the finest on the Camino. I had quail with chickpeas and a glass of sangria, and it helped me forget about my leg pain for the evening. It would return shortly, though, and cause me a great deal of suffering.

I EVENTUALLY BECAME seriously bored with the meseta. I am a little bit embarrassed to say this, as I can usually find *something* to amuse me. "Only boring people get bored" is something I've been known to say. Usually I have the

Rosemary
(Rosmarinus officinalis)

power to adapt to my surroundings as I please, and this time I couldn't do that. I wanted something different, and I wanted the Camino to be pretty again. With the meseta, the Camino goes from quite pretty to quite bland so gradually that I hardly noticed it. From Carrión de los Condes to Terradillos de los Templarios was twenty-seven kilometres! I found that doing twenty to twenty-two kilometres per day suited me perfectly; anything more than that made me grumpy. I really just wanted to get in my truck with a large coffee and speed across the meseta, leaving everyone behind. I was keenly aware of my lack of music and wished badly now that I had brought my iPod with me. I went through all my favourite singers and songs in my head. Dolly Parton, Sara Evans, and Faith Hill were often playing in my brain as I trudged across the land.

The shin splints had got worse again. I'd had no idea previously how painful and debilitating they could be. In fact, before doing the Camino, I had never even heard of a shin splint. It felt like my left shin was locked in a steel trap and there was no way to get it off. I developed a great deal more sympathy for those who run marathons and do long-distance treks. This was the sort of thing they put up with? Unbelievable. It was also very hot in the afternoons, sometimes as much as thirty degrees Centigrade. I find that a very uncomfortable temperature to walk in, so, all in all, the Camino had stopped being fun.

Carol seemed to be taking the meseta in her stride. She had a cute little black umbrella that she was using to keep the sun off her face and she strode merrily along, often chatting with Sandy. On the meseta, I walked more with Isobel than I did with Carol. We talked about movies, books, wildlife, and living in Australia. We talked about our families and our lives, and Isobel's readiness to laugh was something I appreciated.

I made it a point to find fascinating things to look at and hold on to again, but the meseta was ensuring that the plant life got less and less interesting. I did see five deer one morning (from quite a distance) and once a great Spanish bull, standing alone in a field. Curiously, no one else seemed to notice this. The bull sighting was followed, weirdly enough, by a trembling of bullfinches, which came one morning and perched in a large, rambling wild rose covered in scarlet hips. I had never seen bullfinches outside of a book, so that was an exciting moment that helped bring me back to the present. Hedges of Leyland cypress surrounded churches and cemeteries, and their intense and luxurious shade of dark green was a welcome respite from the dry dustbowl we were walking through every day.

Thursday, October 12
Terradillos de los Templarios → Calzada des los Hermanillos

SOME OF THE names of these places were almost as long as the journey. This was the worst day of the Camino for me. We walked twenty-nine *fucking* kilometres, and it was viciously hot for the last four hours we were out there. I did walk alone for most of the day, which was nice, but the shin splints were so extraordinarily painful that it almost defied belief. I began the day grumpy, and by the time we finally got to our albergue I was furious. I tried to hide it as best I could. A decent shower and a sangria helped, and I did see a kingfisher at one point that day. Just a flash of brilliant blue-green over one little nearly dried-up stream I crossed. I swear there is nothing as good for making the heart sing just a little bit as an unexpected bird sighting.

It's mostly cereal crops and grains along the meseta, but we did pass a few smallish vineyards. Sometimes I even saw grape seedlings growing along the ditch, the offspring, no doubt, of occasional clusters of grapes that fell from the wagon during harvest. On this day, I noticed one of these grape vines actually had a bit of fruit on it, which I picked and ate. This was a mistake, as the fruit had become so covered in dust from the road that it was like eating grape-flavoured dirt. I stood there and thought, *I have legitimately tasted the Camino. I have eaten the dust of the road.* It was about as close to a profound thought as I had out there. Well, maybe that's not entirely true.

I use trekking poles for hikes and long walks, and they do a world of good for your knees and joints. I have found, however, that if I hold on to them too tightly, my fingers and hands start to tingle. This happens sometimes when I'm driving too. It occurred to me one day, when this started to happen on the Camino, that there could be other things in my life I hold on to too tightly. Were there things in my life—memories, habits, patterns of behaviour—that I needed to loosen my grip on?

Had it not been suddenly derailed by the sight of a beautiful vegetable garden full of luscious tomatoes, who knows where this train of thought might have taken me? Instead, I started thinking about all the delicious ways tomatoes could be put to use in the kitchen and never did come up with anything I was hanging on to too tightly.

Friday, October 13–Sunday, October 15
Calzada des los Hermanillos → Mansilla de los Mulas → León

I HAVE NEVER walked anywhere where the ground was as rocky as it is on the Camino. Many fields appeared more lunar than European, and it amazed me that this land had probably been ploughed since antiquity, first with horses or oxen and then with machines. The fact that anything grows at all in Spain I found rather remarkable, because most of the soil just appears too full of rocks to ever be able to support life. Yet support life it does, because the crops and the forests and the gardens seemed full of all kinds of different plants and creatures. Places along the meseta that looked too rocky and inhospitable to support flowering plants were often, in fact, generously scattered with flowering plants, in complete defiance of the terrain. I usually look for pollinators as indications of life and health and I often saw sphinx moths feeding in blossoms and there were plenty of honeybees. Strangely, I hardly ever saw beehives. Only twice on the journey did I spot them, and in both instances they looked rather shabby. I wondered where Spain's beekeepers were and what sort of things they would have been able to tell me.

By now, my shin splints had downgraded themselves again from excruciating to just merely uncomfortable. I'm not sure how the body goes about adjusting things so you can continue with your day, but it seems to do exactly that. Sometimes at night I would stretch the wrong way and searing pain would go shooting up my left leg, but during the day, when I walked, it started to get much better. It helped that I had people to walk with, because people can converse with you and offer distraction. I'm always significantly cheerier when I'm not hurting, and since by now we had gotten to know our companions well enough to talk easily with them, I was feeling a lot more myself. Isobel and I often talked about nature or music, and Carol and Sandy and I also found things to discuss. Isobel's husband, Mark, became a source of great amusement to us because every morning he would be the first one to hit the trail and we were always way behind him. "Well, Mark's gone . . ." we would say nearly every morning. We would still be having breakfast and Mark was already three kilometres down the trail.

Most of the people we met along the Camino were lovely and welcoming, with very few exceptions. We met a young English man from Birmingham who became a bit of a problem for us because he showed up frequently and was both amoral and obnoxious. He went on at length about all the ways he could get away with cheating the government and how he had managed to outfox his employer to secure financial rewards he hadn't earned. He was very pleased with himself about this and seemed to want constant validation about how clever he was. While I found him unpleasant, I realized in hindsight that I hadn't been the ideal companion either on the meseta; maybe I had judged him unfairly. When he asked me to join him for a glass of wine in our albergue one evening, I did so. That was a mistake. He started to tell me about "this slag he had been shagging back home," and it got worse from there. I finally had to tell him that there wasn't enough wine in the world for me to sit there and continue listening to him.

There was also a young woman from Russia who I immediately did not like and did not trust, even though everyone else seemed to like her well enough. No one ever really saw her on the trail, and when we arrived at the albergue she was always already there, impeccably dressed, without a speck of dust on her. We began to suspect she was taking a bus or a cab from town to town and only claiming she was a pilgrim. One night I saw her leaving the albergue with a man, and the next night she did the same with a different man. Later, she told me she had found a man to "stay in a hotel with," and I started to suspect she was some kind of a scam artist. Not everyone was on the Camino to find the same thing. . . .

AT LAST, AT the end of the meseta, we entered the thousand-year-old city of León. My shin splints had calmed down enough that I could more or less ignore them, and we walked into the city in high spirits. The path ran alongside a walled, long-forgotten garden. I could see that many trees, including catalpas and paulownias, were behind the crumbling stone wall and wondered what else was hidden back there.

Tree of heaven (famous for being one of the worst weeds in the world and also the titular tree that "grows in Brooklyn") was a common street feature in León, as were tulip trees, magnolias, and lindens. Willows, cedar of Lebanon, and a surprising number of birch trees were also common. I expect that, in the height of summer, León is probably a very green and shady city. When we were there, many of the deciduous trees were already shedding their foliage.

Tulip trees and magnolias are closely related to each other and are among the most ancient flowering plants on earth. Not only do they predate dinosaurs, they actually predate the evolution of bees. Long before bees and flowers had come to a mutually acceptable arrangement, the magnolias were negotiating with beetles. Their flowers are stunning, and their seedpods are clearly from another time period. The climate I live in is too cold and dry for either of these trees, but I have made trips to Vancouver in the spring especially to spend time with them. Of all the flowering trees, magnolias might be the most magnificent and maybe the most mysterious too. I'm always so pleased when I encounter them somewhere, even if they're not in bloom.

LEÓN IS WHERE we had to part with Sandy. She was ending her Camino walk here. This was sad for us, but there was still Glenn and Sue from Texas, who by now were a permanent part of our daily walks, and Mark and Isobel from Australia. Isobel often spoke of our little "Camino family," and we really did take good care of each other. We opted to take another rest day in León, and we stayed in a very cute little apartment hotel run by the most lovely man, whose name was Leo. Leo of León was perhaps in his late thirties and spoke excellent English. He was very cheery and earnest, and we all liked him immediately. He was funny and warm and engaging, if a bit overly friendly. He went into meticulous detail telling us about Kroos, his little dog named for soccer player Toni Kroos, and started telling Carol about his family history (we were quite sure it was going to take four days for him to get out everything he wanted to tell us). In the end, though, he made our stay in León very fun and it made for a nice memory.

We decided, since we'd arrived on a Saturday, to go to a flea market. I have never seen so much junk! Things that should have gone to the landfill two decades before were made available for sale. Hideous old framed paintings from the 1980s, rotary phones, and shabby crucifixes were all priced and laid out for purchase. I couldn't imagine who would want any of this stuff, but perhaps the Spanish are simply much better than we are at reusing and recycling and repurposing things. I don't recall seeing a single landfill in Spain, so there is something to be said for the ability to find value in things that might otherwise have been thrown away.

I have to say that walking around in León nearly killed me. I have never been around so many smokers. Everywhere we went—every outdoor shopping mall, every plaza, every terrace, every busy street—crowds of people were smoking. I am fairly sure I saw at least one person with a cigarette in both hands. It became a source of great irritation for me, because I just wanted to sit down somewhere and enjoy a glass of wine and maybe some tapas. The options were very limited. I started to develop a scratchy throat and a runny nose, and I wasn't sure if I was getting sick or if the smoke was to blame. I decided not to go out the first evening we were there. Instead, I ate an entire bag of Doritos while listening to the ringing of church bells.

The next day, we decided to go and see León's cathedral. It is quite a bit smaller than the cathedral in Burgos, and I was feeling brave. We had been told to visit late in the afternoon, when the low sun would illuminate the exquisite collection of stained glass windows, and to my surprise, the cathedral was . . . delightful. The cathedral in León was built in the thirteenth century and one of its official names translates as "The House of Light." This immediately appealed to me. It is home to one of the largest and best collections of medieval stained glass in all of Europe. Another pilgrim told me the youngest glass in the cathedral was from the 1500s. The only English brochure about it that I could find declared the building to be "a masterpiece of the Gothic style." I took that to mean "this building is old and gorgeous," because I wouldn't know Gothic architecture if I fell through a portal and landed in the midst of it. The cathedral also houses a collection of more than one thousand pieces of sacred art.

Glass and light are two things that are always of interest to me. The way in which glass is made and the ways that we as a species have found to use it are so remarkable! For a (brief) period in my life, shortly after watching a glassblower in Nelson, BC, I determined that I was going to also become a glassblower because it was the most magical and impossible thing I had ever seen. A close friend of mine actually pursued this legitimately at one point, but after a year of trying, she said she had "all but burned off her fingerprints" and still wasn't very good at it. Stained glass windows should be impossible to create, but they aren't.

Something functional, like glass, transformed into art, and that art used to transform the light itself is . . . alchemy.

For me, the stained glass windows in León's "house of light" were about beauty and practicality coming together, and art and function together is almost always a happy marriage. I felt none of the oppression or blackness I had felt in Burgos, and when we stepped outside again, I saw Darwin's barberry (*Berberis darwinii*) planted in large containers along the plaza. This made me smile in spite of the haze of smoke we descended into: after travelling to the past in a cathedral that once housed monks and saints centuries ago, I stepped outside to see a South American shrub first named and collected by Darwin himself. I am sure this pairing was not deliberate, but to me it felt like the history lesson continued. Darwin's findings were at odds with the teachings of the church, and it amused me greatly to see one of his discoveries planted so near to a holy place, and causing no fuss whatsoever. I wondered how many evolutionists and students of Darwin entered the church and found it beautiful, and how many Christians and saints emerged to admire the shining green leaves and beautiful orange flowers of the barberry.

Monday, October 16
León → Villavante

THE DAY WE left León, we were supposed to walk just twenty kilometres to a town called Villar de Mazarife. It was a nice walk. I saw a monkey puzzle tree as we were leaving the city, and behind a wall I saw the distinct feathery branches and reddish flowers of a pride of Barbados (*Caesalpinia pulcherrima*), the only one I saw in Spain. There were more beautiful vegetable gardens and zinnias and roses and lots of gladioli and dahlias. I saw a lot of dahlias in Spain.

When we got to the little albergue we were supposed to stay at, Carol and I checked in and did what we always did upon arrival: looked for bedbugs. Bedbugs have become a significant problem in the modern world, and rural northern Spain is not an exception. We met several people on the Camino who had been severely bitten during the night, and so Carol and I vowed we would never stay anywhere where bedbugs were a problem. Before leaving home, I had educated myself as much as possible on what they look like, what their habits are, and where to find them, and Carol and I were very scrupulous about checking for them everywhere we stayed.

As luck would have it, this time we found a bedbug in Carol's bunk. We got the woman who had checked us in to come to the room and showed her the little insect, which was reclining on the pillow like it owned the place. She immediately moved us to another room. Carol and I checked it thoroughly and found nothing, but still we didn't feel exactly safe. "I don't want to stay here," I told Carol. She didn't want to either. Neither of us was going to get any rest in a place where we were worried about bugs (*chinches* in Spanish) crawling over us and biting us. The woman gave us our money back straight away and hurried us out the door lest we inform any other guest that there might be a problem.

There was only one other albergue in town. Carol and I checked into that one, went upstairs to our room, and immediately discovered another bedbug. It was the only time on the entire Camino that we found them, and so we repeated what had just happened, got our money back, and left. We found Mark and Isobel and Glenn and Sue and told them what was going on. They were staying in the first albergue in rooms on a different floor. They had thoroughly checked their rooms as well and did not have any issues.

Carol and I debated what to do. The next town, Villavante, was another ten kilometres away. Ten kilometres is a negligible distance if you are driving; on foot, when you have already been walking all day, it is very far indeed. I said to Carol, "This is bullshit! Call us a cab and I'll pay for it." Carol did manage to get through to a cab company. Always polite and well mannered, she did her best to explain, partly in English and partly in Spanish, where we were. We weren't sure exactly what the problem was, but the cab company told us, essentially, that wherever we were, it was unknown to them. I started laughing hysterically now, because the situation was ridiculous. In what country in the world were cabs just not available?

We had a good laugh about the absurdity of it and then decided we had no choice. We walked the extra ten or eleven kilometres to Villavante, making our tally for the day a full thirty kilometres. It was the longest day I had on the Camino, and when we got to the next albergue, I was sure I would burst into tears if we also found bedbugs there. Thankfully, we did not, and we had a deep and peaceful rest.

Tuesday, October 17–Wednesday, October 18
Villavante → Hospital del Órbigo → Astorga

THE FOLLOWING DAY, we left for Hospital del Órbigo. Once upon a time, there was actually a pilgrim's hospital here, and this is how the town got its name. This may not have been a hospital in the sense that we might think of it, but rather a church or hostel where one could receive medical attention if needed. Several times on our route we passed cemeteries or graveyards where the names and dates on the stones had long since worn away. A pilgrim from the Czech Republic told me that, in days of old, many people actually died on the Camino and those unmarked stones were for "pilgrims who didn't make it." They were ill-prepared for the journey, in either health or clothing or both. The church felt it was important that priests be available to administer last rites to those who were unlikely to make it to Santiago. The Spanish crown protected these hospitals, and pilgrims were encouraged to make donations to help pay for food or medical treatment they received there.

Hospital del Órbigo sits on the banks of the Órbigo River, and you must cross a gorgeous stone bridge to enter the town. When we crossed, I noticed fish were jumping in the water below. Gardens were full of vegetables and many flowers, including gaillardia, oleander, zinnias, dahlias, gladioli, callas, lavender, and even bacopa. Mint and lemon balm grew abundantly as well, and once again fig and walnut trees were plentiful.

Zinnias were named for the German botanist Johann Zinn but were first brought to Europe in the 1500s by the Spanish. It pleased me to see them so often in so many places wherever we went. Fast growing and easily hybridized, zinnias are members of the enormous daisy family and come in almost every conceivable colour. They can be short or tall, with small or large flowers, and they bloom for months with little care or attention. Zinnias are the first flower I can remember growing from seed. I was five, and I remember my mother filling my hands with what looked like a handful of brown dust. We sprinkled that dust into the earth, and tiny green shoots began to emerge a few days later. Soon those shoots were producing stems and leaves, and then buds. Every day there were changes. The buds soon opened to immense, cushion-like flowers I could almost recline on. Their colours were so bright I could practically taste them. I often credit those zinnias with helping to make sure that I grew up to be a gardener. Zinnias are an old friend. I have seen them in many nations and admired them in the gardens of both the rich and the poor. I wondered for how many generations those zinnias had been brightening the path of travellers.

We got there at about noon, checked into a very nice albergue that had a distinct hippie vibe to it, and decided that we would have a bit of a rest day, as Carol and I had more than exceeded the usual distance on the previous day. The albergue reminded me of being in Byron Bay in Australia or Nelson in British Columbia. The staff were extremely nice, but I found myself melancholy and sad when we got there. I was seriously missing home and my family, and I just wanted a very large coffee and the company of an old friend. I wasn't sure what I was even doing out on the Camino. A nice Australian girl named Marie was staying at the albergue, and she and I bonded a little bit since she was feeling much the same way.

There were lots of books available in the albergue, but most of them were in Spanish. It is fortunate that scientific names are universal, as I found a book about plants of the Camino and was able to make some notes. This actually proved to be extremely helpful. From this book, I identified about half a dozen things that I had seen along the trail but previously did not recognize. First was a tall white umbellifer that grew in all the ditches, and the book identified it as *Angelica sylvestris*. I had not expected it to be an angelica, but I should have. The sea holly whose seed heads I saw every day was *Eryngium campestre*, and the weedy looking knapweed with the pinkish flowers was *Centaurea calcitrapa*.

Perhaps the most useful identification was that of a beautiful plant with spires of golden daisy-like flowers that I had come to love. It often grew in large numbers, and I thought it was very pleasing to the eye in both colour and shape, but I didn't know what it was. The book called it the herb of St. James (*hierba de Santiago* in Spanish) and identified it as a species of *Senecio*, which I had guessed but not been certain of. Part of the daisy family, this beautiful plant produces an extraordinary amount of nectar, making it of great importance to bees and butterflies. It is also a very common weed and is generally disregarded, despite its showy displays of golden blooms. It grows throughout Europe and was once widely regarded as a medicinal plant, particularly for wounds and injuries related to walking long distances. Early Christians said it was planted by St. James himself to provide medicine for weary travellers as they journeyed to his resting place.

This was the only albergue we stayed at that was vegetarian. It also had a greenhouse, and in the evening I went to snoop about in it. It was well kept, but there was dog shit all over the floor, which grossed me out and kind of lessened the appeal of the "organic garden" that the hostel boasted about on the sign outside. Nonetheless, we were served one of the most beautiful meals of the entire Camino that night: a delicious salad of kale, fresh tomatoes, and balsamic vinegar, a totally vegetarian shepherd's pie, and dessert. Everyone was well fed and happy, and I felt a lot more relaxed than I had earlier in the day. Even better, a woman who worked there was a qualified masseuse, and for a small fee I got a wonderful foot and leg massage. Everyone went off to bed contented and peaceful, including myself. There was nothing to indicate any trouble was to come.

USUALLY, I WAS one of the first to fall asleep every night, but on this particular night . . . oh dear. I had been in bed for about an hour, and my stomach was really starting to hurt.

I tried to ignore it and just sleep. I told myself I had just eaten too much. By 11:00 p.m., my stomach was insisting that I get up and do something. I hauled myself out of bed, crept through the darkened room full of sleeping pilgrims, found the men's bathroom, and totally woofed my cookies.

I hate throwing up. I will go out of my way to avoid having to do it. The worst thing for me about having the flu is throwing up.

And I am a scream-puker.

If you are not familiar with this terminology, let me lay it out for you. Some human beings are capable of barfing very quietly, discreetly even. They can slip into the loo, relieve their stomach of all its contents, and slip back out with no one being the wiser. This is not a skill I have. Before the vomit actually comes out of them, scream-pukers (and you know who you are) must involuntarily scream as if participating in some sort of ritual ceremony in a cult. We go "aaaaauuuuggghhhhhh!!!" before our stomach is willing to expel whatever nasty thing it is dealing with. I hadn't thrown up like this since I was very young. I had to hold on to the toilet bowl to brace myself while these *Exorcist*-like streams of vomit flowed out of me.

After this horrifying little escapade, I felt a bit better and went back to bed. This was at about 11:00 p.m., and at midnight there was a repeat performance. At 1:10, I went back to vomit some more, and again at 2:20. I kept track. Between the hours of 11:00 p.m. and 7:00 a.m., I scream-puked eleven times. That would have been bad enough, but several times, in addition to the vomiting, I also had to shit like a T-Rex. Each time, I prayed ferociously to every saint I'd encountered on the journey to please let me not have to do both at the same time.

I was sure my scream-puking had woken every single person in the albergue, but literally no one was disturbed.

In fact, in the weeks that followed, my travelling companions kept commenting on just how calm and tranquil that albergue had been. At breakfast, Mark asked me, "How are you today?" and I cheerfully announced that I felt like complete shit. No one asked any follow-up questions, which annoyed me, not because I wanted sympathy but because everyone else was talking about what a wonderful meal and sleep they'd had and wasn't everything just terrific? There is nothing more annoying when you are sick than people talking about how good they feel. So even though I was dehydrated and exhausted and in no shape to do anything physical, we walked fourteen kilometres that day, much of it in the rain. I was cold and miserable the entire way.

No one else became ill, so I assume it was a virus or tummy bug I'd picked up somewhere, rather than food poisoning. I threw up twice on the trail that day and didn't eat anything for almost two days. It was the only day on the Camino when I don't remember looking at any plants. Part of that walk was right beside the highway, with big trucks flying past, and I really just wanted an armchair, a fireplace, a pot of tea, and to be far away from people. I feel like I accomplished something, though. Ever since then, when I am in a tight situation, I will say to myself, "Remember that time on the Camino when you were sick as a dog and you still managed to walk fourteen kilometres in the rain?" That's a pretty boss thing to do. I am tougher than I realized.

WHEN WE WALKED into Astorga, I was still so miserable I barely noticed the beautiful mountain views that were starting to come up. I was barely aware of the musician playing welcoming music on his violin. I felt chilly right down to my bones. When we got to our albergue, I spent another very unpleasant twenty-five minutes in the bathroom and cursed the Camino and Spain and myself for having left home. Then I went to bed to "convalesce."

I didn't go out to dinner that night, and our albergue was very quiet. I did meet a sweet couple from New Zealand who told me that, whatever it was I was dealing with, they'd had the same thing a few days earlier. It was reassuring to know that I hadn't contracted some virulent new disease. By the following morning, I was able to eat a little bit and was starting to feel better.

Thursday, October 19–Friday, October 20
Astorga → Rabanal del Camino → El Acebo de San Miguel

ALL ALONG THE way to Rabanal del Camino, where we stopped on the night of October 19, there were black elderberries growing in the ditch. Their clusters of shiny black fruits, which admittedly were covered in dust, were so abundant they almost looked like flowers. I thought it was very appropriate to be met with bouquets of black blooms following what I am sure was a brush with near death. (I'm overly dramatic sometimes.)

After the monotony of the meseta, I was amazed at how exquisite the landscape became again after Astorga. We were crossing into the lush, rainy region of Galicia, the greenest corner of Spain. Forests of oak and pine with great blankets of bracken fern spreading out beneath them became the norm. Mysterious blue-green mountains in the distance started to become visible, and once more there were great towering oak trees. I figured out that they were most likely Pyrenean oaks (*Quercus pyrenaica*), and their acorns once again littered the ground. Hawthorn, bird cherry, birch, and mountain ash also became common as

we continued to make our way west to Santiago. The next day, on the road from Rabanal del Camino to El Acebo de San Miguel, I discovered one of the most beautiful chestnut trees I had ever seen. Chestnuts are relatives of the oaks, and I was aware of their existence, but the Camino was the first time I really had the opportunity to observe them up close and personal.

SWEET CHESTNUTS (*CASTANEA*) should not be confused with horse chestnuts (*Aesculus*). Both are common throughout Europe. There are twelve species of sweet chestnut, and they are native to Europe, North America, and northern Asia, with many species being ornamental as well as useful. Well-drained, acidic soil with good moisture conditions suits them best. They are unfortunately not prairie hardy; the very toughest of them might survive in zone 4 or 5. If I lived somewhere that they would grow, I would definitely consider planting one. The nuts have been a food source for thousands of years. Alexander the Great and the ancient Romans planted them widely, and the Greek physician and botanist Dioscorides not only wrote of them, he complained that overindulging in them made him flatulent. In France and Italy they have been known for generations and were often disregarded as being the food of the poor.

The American chestnut (*Castanea dentata*) was once one of the most widely planted, most loved trees in North America. Although the flowers have an unpleasant smell, the tree produces gorgeous dark-green foliage and very large, delicious nuts held in prickly burs. The nuts fall when ripe. Because it casts a dense and heavy shade, it was considered an ideal tree for parks. Sadly, the American chestnut has been all but wiped out. In the early 1900s, chestnut blight was discovered in New York State. It spread from there and quickly wiped out nearly every American chestnut on the continent. A few still exist, but they are badly infected and are only just clinging to life. Researchers continued to look for a cure into the 1930s, but no real progress was ever made. European species are largely immune to this malady, and efforts have been made to produce hybrid offspring that contain the best traits of both and none of the disease susceptibility. Thus far, these efforts have not been completely successful.

The Spanish chestnut (*Castanea sativa*), the species I encountered on my journey, comes from southern Europe and western Asia. It is a gorgeous and fast-growing tree that reaches sixty feet. The delicious nuts are considered a delicacy. Many hybrids have been developed. These are the chestnuts of commerce, with 'Colossal,' 'Nevada,' and

'Schrader' being the best-known cultivars. They produce larger nuts than either of their parents, and they are also more vigorous and produce bigger crops. They are sometimes planted as ornamentals, and their brilliant yellow fall colour is quite beautiful.

Chestnuts are very nutritious and are peculiar in being the only nuts known to contain vitamin C; they are also self-sterile, incapable of pollinating their own blossoms. To obtain a crop, two trees must be grown reasonably close together. Sicily is currently the world's leading supplier of chestnuts, but France and Portugal also produce a large quantity.

The horse chestnuts (*Aesculus*) and their American relations, the buckeyes, are not related to the true chestnuts. The common name is a corruption of "coarse" chestnut, and they were so called to distinguish them from sweet chestnuts. No species in this genus produces edible nuts. These are slow-growing, wide-spreading trees that can reach significant sizes and are found in nearly every major city in Europe. They cast a heavy shade and are ideal for front yards or parks. Their candle-like flower clusters in the spring are very ornamental, and their large, stone-like reddish brown seeds cover streets and sidewalks in the fall. All have beautiful foliage: the leaves are divided into numerous leaflets, somewhat resembling a hand. The seedpods are prickly and split open when fully ripe to reveal shiny, smooth, rather beautiful seeds. (Squirrels will eat these; humans will not.) The prickly husks are painful if stepped on in bare feet, and the British know them as "conkers." All of these trees are easy to cultivate, but they do grow from a taproot and are very cranky about being disturbed. They are prone to suffering long bouts of transplant shock and should be planted as small as possible, ideally as seed. Sowing the fresh seed in fall generally results in germination the following spring.

A rich, fertile soil with good moisture conditions will suit them, though they are extremely drought-tolerant once established. Furthermore, they are very prone to windburn, particularly when young, and if at all possible should be planted in a sheltered site. Horse chestnuts are often the last trees to leaf out in the spring and are not subject to pests or disease, and they rarely need any pruning. They are much planted on both the east and west coasts but little seen on the prairies.

By far the hardiest species in the family are the European horse chestnut (*A. hippocastanum*) and the Ohio buckeye (*A. glabra*). European horse chestnut is officially hardy to zone 4. It can reach sixty feet in height and is native mainly to Albania and northern Greece at high elevations. The cream-coloured to ivory flowers are produced in great profusion, then comes a huge crop of the famously inedible nuts. Although this species is not well suited to the prairies, mature and stunning examples of these trees can be found in Edmonton, Camrose, and Calgary. In most cases, they were grown from seed and nurtured and pampered until they were able to adapt to the climate.

Ohio buckeye is the state tree of Ohio, and as the name implies, it is native to central and eastern North America. It can grow into a very large tree of fifty to sixty feet, but it is slow growing and infrequently planted. The large leaves are quite splendid and although the blossoms are not as showy or profuse as *A. hippocastanum*, they are still certainly attractive. The large clusters of seeds that follow provide food for squirrels and deer. The seed is an enormous roundish ball that ranges from reddish brown to dark brown. It is encased in a prickly husk about the size of a walnut, and as they ripen, the husks start to break open, revealing the large, shiny seed inside. With a little imagination, one could imagine it was the dark-brown eye of a deer peering out at you, hence the common name of buckeye. The seeds are so smooth and polished-looking that I keep a bowl of them here on my desk just to be decorative. Sometimes I pick them up and marvel at their beauty. The trees' fall colour is highly variable: yellow is the usual, but orange and red are not unheard of, and some years they produce no bright fall colour at all. Both of these trees are easily grown from fresh seed sown in the fall, and mature specimens exist in Saskatoon, Regina, Calgary, and Edmonton.

AFTER FINDING THE most beautiful chestnut tree of the entire Camino, we were walking down a high road when a group of teenagers, who were on a school trip, came along the path. It didn't take long for several of the girls to start shrieking and freaking out about something on the road. I went to investigate and found a dead fire salamander that had been run over. That was bad enough, but then I realized there were actually quite a number of them. Having grown up on the prairie with tiger salamanders and being fond of them, it made me sad to find their European relatives squished along the road. It also made me think about my work in Waterton Lakes National Park, where the only "salamander crossing" sign in all of Canada may be found.

If you remember any scene at all from *Macbeth*, it might be the three witches around their cauldron. You may also remember that one of the ingredients in their potion was "eye of newt." Those of us who grew up in North America would mostly know newts as salamanders. All newts are salamanders, but not all salamanders are newts. The differences between the two are subtle, but salamanders tend to be more terrestrial and newts tend to be more aquatic. The tails of newts are more "fin-like," used to propel and steer them while they swim. Salamanders have this feature in their larval stage but do not retain it into adulthood. Many newts also produce toxins in their skin as a way of avoiding being eaten by predators.

The fire salamander is often referred to as a newt and can be found in central European forests, usually in hilly areas. They like to hide in fallen leaves and in mossy places, generally in areas where moisture is abundant. Chestnut forests are good places to look for them, since chestnuts like moisture themselves.

BEFORE REACHING OUR next stop, in El Acebo de San Miguel, we had to pass near the Cruz de Fierro ("the iron cross"), which is said to be the highest point on the Camino. One of the Camino traditions is for each pilgrim to take with them on their journey a rock or stone from home and to leave it behind here, at Cruz de Fierro. The idea is that you are physically letting go of something, and that this is a symbol of the letting go of other, less tangible, things. Maybe something emotional, spiritual, or intellectual. I had brought three little crystalline stones from the coulees of Lethbridge to leave behind. I wasn't really sure what to expect or what I would find, but I thought it was certainly a neat idea.

When we got to this interesting, even iconic, spot, we found a very large hill made up of things that pilgrims have left behind. I was amazed at the sheer number of pilgrims milling about. I had a good look around and deposited my three little stones in the pile. Carol asked me to take a picture of her. I found the show of emotion going on around me somewhat surprising. Many people were sitting and meditating in the sun, others were openly weeping, still others were sitting around in small groups talking quietly, and some were holding hands and staring at the iron cross. I don't know why, but I felt like the sentimentality was out of place and rather off-putting. It reminded me of my involuntary reaction to the gold-drenched cathedral at Burgos, and I got the heck out of there pretty fast, although not as fast as I had left the cathedral.

When we arrived in El Acebo de San Miguel that day, we stayed in what was possibly the nicest albergue of the entire trip. It was sort of like a high-end hotel: very, very clean, with spectacular views and a wonderful little bar where we ate a delicious cake and drank sangrias. The rooms were spacious and large, and there were showers/bathrooms that were huge and spotlessly clean and modern. The staff were excellent. We shared our room that night with a nice Korean couple, and we put our shoes out on the balcony for the night because they did not smell good. Of course it *poured* that night and in the morning our shoes were *drenched*. Carol took her shoes and mine to the ladies bathroom because there was an insanely large hairdryer thing in there. She spent forty-five minutes drying her shoes and mine before we left in the morning so that we didn't have to walk in wet shoes!

Saturday, October 21
El Acebo de San Miguel → Ponferrada

THE NEXT DAY took us about sixteen kilometres to Ponferrada. I have to say that I really enjoyed Ponferrada. Although not nearly as large as Burgos or León, it is an attractive and welcoming place, with Chinese fan palms and lots of flowers and some impressive eucalyptus trees.

By this point on our journey, the season was definitely changing. Summer had given way to autumn, and autumn was whispering about winter. Mornings were cold; I had to buy a toque and gloves. There was evidence of frost. Once the sun came up, however, it was reasonably warm again each day, and one thing we wanted to see in Ponferrada was the Templar's castle. It turned out to be one of my favourite things on the whole Camino.

This enormous castle is of great significance to the Camino for several reasons. It was built in 1178 by King Ferdinand II of León and given to the Knights Templar. They were charged with protecting the pilgrims who passed through on their way to Santiago, and according to my limited understanding, it functioned as a base of operations for these important peacekeepers and guardians. For about twenty years, the Templars did their job, and then the order was disbanded and all their properties ended up in the hands of the Spanish crown. It's now a major tourist destination, and restoration works are ongoing.

Hilariously, I almost missed the castle's massive front gate because I was distracted by the lushest planting of box honeysuckle (*Lonicera nitida*) I have ever encountered, which grew all around the base of the exterior. Once inside the imposing stone building, I found a superb exhibit that included ancient textbooks and paintings of European birds and mushrooms. It was all laid out beautifully, with very helpful signage in several languages. But apart from that and the castle's history, impressive size, and beautiful stonework, I loved that it looked just as I imagined a medieval castle should look. I loved the towers and turrets and the bridge that led to the main door. I loved how it took up a significant portion of the town and insisted on being noticed and admired. My inner eight-year-old, who imagined fighting dragons and rescuing princesses, *adored* it.

I would have been happy with this castle, quite fully happy and not in need of anything else, but just across the beautiful cobbled road from this great, monolithic work of stone was another kind of work of art. People who know me or have attended my classes may be aware of my overwhelming fondness for the great purple majesty that is the wisteria vine. Under the right circumstances, wisterias can live for centuries. The brilliant Irish writer Thomas Pakenham has even suggested that wisterias are closer to trees than mere woody vines. He may well be correct.

Living just across the way from the castle was the largest wisteria I have ever seen. It was undoubtedly at least a century old, but probably more. A trunk thicker than my waist supported the bulk of this exquisite specimen, and a series of metal props allowed her to recline suggestively against a beautiful stone wall. Seedpods dangled elegantly from her branches, hinting at a banquet for bees earlier in the year. The wisteria embraced the entire building, holding court over a river that flows beside the castle, where I like to think she has been admired and greatly loved since time immemorial. I wondered how many souls she has brought joy to over the hundreds of years she has been lounging here in the Spanish sun. Wisterias are mostly native to China and Japan, and someone must have planted her here not long after the plant was first made available to Western gardeners. I wondered what blessed monk first planted her in this fertile soil and if they knew what effect she would have. I like to personify plants, and I feel strongly that this wisteria is a she. I've never seen a better example of this plant before, and for the rest of my life I will fondly remember Ponferrada, with its castle, its beautiful rolling views of mountains, and the wisteria at its heart.

Sunday, October 22
Ponferrada → Villafranca del Bierzo

AFTER THE DRY, dusty meseta, it was so nice once again to be walking somewhere *pretty*. From Ponferrada, our next stop was Villafranca del Bierzo. We walked through absolutely gorgeous vineyards with blue-green mountains in the distance that were draped with mist and low-hanging clouds. The cracks in old stone walls were filled with sedums and a peculiar plant that was some kind of *Umbilicus*. It had circular, fleshy leaves and an unusual look about it. The walls were also home to licorice ferns and lichens, and I wondered how old the stones were and how they got to where they were. Dragged on a cart by mules, perhaps.

As we walked, we kept hearing the loud echo of a gunshot in the distance and caught the occasional sight of someone moving through the vineyards with a dog. I assume they were hunting rabbits, as I saw a number of them trying to hide on the edges of the path. I don't know whether they were being hunted for food or as vermin; I imagine rabbits could be very destructive to grape vines. If they were being eaten, I wouldn't be surprised by that either; one night I had very nice roast rabbit in a restaurant. In addition to the vineyards, pears and quinces were hung with ripe fruit, and the quinces in particular were very beautiful.

The quince (*Cydonia oblonga*) is the only species in its genus and is closely related to the pear. Fruits are large, golden-yellow, and often slightly misshapen-looking at maturity. They are hard as a stone and are not eaten raw but are cooked or preserved in some way first. Quince jelly and candied quinces are prized food items in many parts of Europe. Historically, this tree has also been celebrated for its attractive pink flowers in the spring and for the shade it provides.

Strongly aromatic at peak ripeness, quinces were once set out in bowls to scent rooms in people's houses and in churches and monasteries. They smell of pears, but more sweetly. In the wild, quince has a very wide distribution throughout the southwestern parts of Asia, Turkey, Iran, and Afghanistan. It often grows in rocky soil and is very adaptable. The ancient Greeks made it sacred to Aphrodite, and the fruit was often preserved in honey or wine or both. A hot summer will produce the best-quality fruit, and the amount of fruit produced can be significant.

The Spanish call the quince *membrillo,* and I saw it quite a lot in gardens and for sale in markets. In one restaurant we ate in, quince cheese was offered as the dessert, a regional specialty. I didn't find it especially delicious, but I might feel differently if I had grown up with the fruit as a regular part of my diet. The trees with their golden fruit were certainly gorgeous to look at.

LATE SUMMER AND early fall may not be the best time for flowers on the Camino, but it was certainly a good time for fruit and vegetables. On several occasions towards the end of the journey, we saw fields full of pumpkins. In many cases, these were unusually shaped or unusually coloured, and I suspect they were old heirloom types that have been grown for a century or more. Several restaurants offered pumpkin soup, which was among the more delicious things we ate in Spain. The sight of a field of pumpkins always makes me extraordinarily happy; there is something so cheery and uplifting about these great glowing orbs that appear at summer's end. Red peppers began to show up more and more as well, and we often saw them drying on tables or hung on long strings. Roasted red pepper sauce came up as an item on a few of our pilgrim menus and it

was delicious. There were also long strings of some of the most robust-looking garlic I've ever seen, and one restaurant served us a garlic soup (*sopa de ajo*) that was absolutely outstanding.

As we got farther into Galicia, we saw many large plantings of a very upright, very lush plant with prominent blue-green leaves. It was obviously something in the cabbage family, but what? It took me a day or two to realize that it was walking stick cabbage. Also called Jersey cabbage, cow cabbage, and tree cabbage, this is a very old heirloom from Jersey in the Channel Islands. It needs a growing season of about 180 days, making it difficult, but not impossible, to grow on the prairies. Northern Spain is obviously the perfect climate for it, and Galician soup often featured this stalwart and hardy vegetable. To those of us who think cabbage always has a dense head, it is a strange-looking variety. It rapidly grows straight up, producing a lightweight, very solid "trunk" as it develops. These sticks can be cut, carved, and varnished to make walking sticks. While the leaves are certainly edible, they are much tougher than most cabbages or kales. For this reason, they are almost always cooked and rarely eaten raw. The average walking stick cabbage will grow about six feet tall, but occasionally they reach as much as nine feet (the world record is eighteen!). One morning, as we walked I saw an old woman in her vegetable garden. She was wearing an earthy-brown sweater and had a wide basket full of cabbage leaves. The contrast of the nearly blue foliage with her reddish-brown wool sweater was very memorable. I watched her for a moment as she deftly plucked the leaves from the plant, and then she went back inside her little house when the basket was full.

I was amazed at how many flowers, plants, and gardens I saw on this section of the trail. Pots full of marigolds, petunias, and ivy geraniums were common. I saw hostas, impatiens, hollyhocks, and callas in many gardens and containers as well. Hydrangeas, birch, and holly were abundant, as were almond and peach trees (though the season for peaches was long past). I even saw some very large prickly pear cactuses with mauve-coloured fruit. I wondered if the Spanish eat them or if they are grown purely for ornamental purposes.

ONE OF THE best reasons to travel is to try foods that are unlike what you'd find at home. Ask anyone about their trip to Japan, Thailand, or Italy, and they will immediately begin telling you about the delicious things they ate while they were there. Before going on the Camino, I did some research into Spanish cuisine. My findings were that the best food in Spain and the most "authentic" Spanish culinary delights were to be found in Seville, Barcelona, and Madrid. These were not places we would be walking through. Pilgrims who had gone before me described the fare along the Camino as "often bland." One person called it "uninspiring." Since I will eat pretty much anything and I don't have any food allergies or dietary restrictions, I was determined to try any new or fascinating food I found along the way. Another factor when walking the Camino, of course, is that the physical demands of the walk mean that you are constantly hungry, so pretty much anything you find to eat is good enough. Wine is abundant in Spain, and Europe in general is well known for its delicious cheeses. Wine and cheese nights at home are a mild extravagance; on the Camino, wine and cheese are just food.

Towards the end of our trek across Spain, I began to notice a rather unusually shaped cheese in a lot of the shops. Instead of the typical wheel or brick shape, these were more like very broad teardrops. "They're shaped like breasts," someone said, when I mentioned this. I suppose they *are* breast-shaped. I hadn't considered that. It turns out that locals call this *quesc gallego de Tetilla*, or sometimes *queso de pecho*, which translates loosely as "breast cheese." It's a Galician cow's-milk cheese, but there's a story behind it, as there often is on the Camino.

When one passes from the grand entrance stairway into the Cathedral of St. James in Santiago, there is a portico filled with statues and carvings of biblical figures. Specifically, there is a group of men representing several Old Testament prophets. Most of them look very solemn, but one prophet, curiously, is smiling. One might even say leering. If you turn around, you'll see what he is smiling about. Across from him stands a statue of the biblical Queen Esther. As originally sculpted, she was gloriously bare-chested, with her great bosom on full display. Then, in the fifteenth century, along came a very pious archbishop who was scandalized that such a sight should be seen by pilgrims coming to the church to pray. He issued an order to have the beautiful queen's ample stone breasts chiselled off. Local dairy farmers, enraged at what they considered the desecration of a holy place, began making their cheeses in the shape of breasts as a sign of their disapproval. So popular was this protest that cheese continues to be made in this shape to the present day.

Fast-forward a few centuries, and here I am out on the Camino trail. The day after I had had the chance to sample one of these cheeses (which turned out to be very mild in flavour, but good all the same) thanks to the thoughtfulness of our friends Glenn and Sue, I ran into a group of four American women who were walking just a small section of the Camino while on holiday. I found myself in a conversation with them and soon deduced they were very devout and were viewing the Camino in a very sombre way. Well, that was fine, until one of them brought up the oddly shaped local cheeses and I told them the story about the Queen Esther statue.

Rather than being amused, they were horrified. Not horrified that the queen's body parts had been hacked off, but horrified at the idea of a nude depiction of an important biblical figure. One of them felt strongly that the archbishop had done the right thing. Something came over me and I countered with, "Yes, but doesn't the Bible say blessed are the cheesemakers?" This was met with strange looks and stony silence. Finally, one of them said, without a trace of humour, "No, it says blessed are the *peace*makers." I smiled: "I know that. I was making a little joke." More stony silence. "That isn't funny," one of them said at last. "Really? It's not?" I said. "Because I think it's hilarious."

Not surprisingly, the conversation ended and I resumed the rest of the journey to Villafranca del Bierzo with my usual group.

Monday, October 23
Villafranca del Bierzo → Las Herrerías

THE LONG TWENTY-FIVE-KILOMETRE haul to Las Herrerías was our next section of the trail. It started with a very steep uphill climb before sunrise, and when the sun finally came up we had spectacular mountain views.

We were walking through forests of birch and pine. These gave way to chestnuts, which were excessively beautiful. As I said earlier, chestnuts do not grow well in my part of the world, and encountering them in the forest in a natural setting was particularly wonderful for me. The trees were dropping their prickly green burs that hold the large russet-coloured seeds, and huge quantities of chestnuts covered the forest floor. They were like gems spilling from a treasure chest. I walked alone for a good part of the day, quietly experiencing the particular joys of a chestnut forest.

The Japanese have a beautiful word—*komorebi*—for the patterns that the sunlight makes on the forest floor as it filters down through the canopy. The patterns created by the chestnut trees, with their long leaves and corrugated bark, were captivating. Another unusual characteristic of a chestnut forest is its quietness: chestnut leaves do not rustle in the wind the same way that many other trees do, and I found the chestnut forests exquisitely silent except for the occasional singing of a titmouse or robin.

THOUGH YOU PRETTY much walk all day on the Camino, you do stop from time to time along the way for a rest or a coffee or sometimes an ice-cream cone. We always looked forward to our first coffee stop of the day, but on this day, my morning walk through chestnut forests had me so elated, I almost forgot to stop at the next tiny village.

I'm glad I did. It was little more than a modest collection of houses, but it had a café, and the delightful woman who ran it offered up chestnut cake. She had made it herself, she was able to convey, and it was a speciality. As near as we could figure out, chestnut cake is made by roasting the nuts and then grinding them into a kind of flour. It was delicious. She also made us sandwiches for the road, with big slices of freshly picked tomatoes, which were outstanding. She must have had a real interest in gardening, because her containers held things I hadn't seen in most places. She had a large tub of orchid cactus (*Epiphyllum*) spilling over on her upper balcony, several tubs of hens and chicks, and some really gorgeous, luminous, yellow evening primroses. Someone had planted a screen of bamboo, and red peppers were being dried in a shed. Everything was very neat and tidy. I wished I could have talked more with her, but despite the language barrier, I think we did manage to communicate.

When we were on our way again through the last part of the chestnut-filled forest, on more than one occasion I met an elderly local emerging from the shadows with a basket of freshly gathered chestnuts. I wondered how many decades of their lives they had been going into the woods to do this, and if they enjoyed it, and what they thought of the endless parade of pilgrims that they must see every year.

Tuesday, October 24
Las Herrerías → Fonfría

THE FOLLOWING DAY, we again walked through mountain forest. The chestnuts continued, but here the forest became more diverse. We encountered alder and gorse, broom and Scotch pine, heathers and birch and oaks. Sometimes I saw white or red chrysanthemums in bloom in gardens, and very often there were great companies of walking stick cabbage. We knew when we had officially crossed the border into Galicia, because immediately we could smell silage. I am not a fan of how it smells, and I now understood what people on the Internet meant when they referred to "the distinctive odour" of Galicia.

We passed through O Cebreiro, a striking and picturesque little village that you come to after a steep and somewhat treacherous uphill climb. The village is famous, in part because Don Elias was born there. He was the priest I mentioned earlier who was responsible for the yellow arrows and waymarkers along the route. Several busloads of tourists were milling about, but the place still managed to seem a little mysterious and forgotten. Galicia is often called the most Celtic part of Spain, and one hears bagpipes and sees low stone walls with mists clinging to them and can easily picture Scotland or Ireland or Wales. Many of the buildings in O Cebreiro were covered in ivy, something I had seen a lot of on my journey.

What could be more European than great bowers of ivy? I saw ivy everywhere, and I loved it. It rambled through the woods and up into trees and over old sheds. It was climbing up barns and making its way along the walls of abandoned churches and creeping into long-forgotten buildings.

All true species of ivy belong in the genus *Hedera,* and they are native throughout Europe, northern Africa, and parts of Japan and Taiwan. There are fifteen recognized species and many subspecies. All are evergreen, rampant vines that may also become groundcovers. Flowering normally occurs from autumn through winter. The flowers are small and inconspicuous but have a strong fragrance. This scent is not altogether pleasant, but it draws flurries of bees at a time of the year when they have very little else to be foraging in. The European ivy bee (*Colletes hederae*) pollinates *Hedera helix* exclusively, and the lifecycle of the bee revolves entirely around the blooming of this one plant. I passed a number of ivies in bloom and looked for their small, industrious little friend, but I'm not sure that I saw one. I may have, but they look similar to honeybees and I couldn't tell. Small black berries, eaten by birds, follow the blossoms. These berries are mildly toxic and can make humans quite ill.

Ivies hybridize very freely and there is also a huge degree of genetic variation even in a single population. *Hedera helix* is the English ivy that creeps up walls and trees and buildings throughout the British Isles and much of Europe. It is a plant of abundant shapes and textures. Its leaves can variously be green, variegated, heart-shaped, finely cut, triangular, splashed with gold, fan-shaped, ruffled, heavily crisped, large, or very tiny. In places where ivy is not hardy, it is frequently cultivated as a houseplant, as an annual for baskets and containers, especially in shady areas, and often added to wedding bouquets.

Outside of its natural range, ivy has become an invasive species in many places. It can climb forty or fifty feet into a tree and smother everything in its path. It has been blamed for the death of large trees because of the weight it adds and because its evergreen cover provides the perfect breeding ground for insects, mildews, and moulds. Birds eat the berries and distribute the seeds in their droppings. The hardiest forms of ivy come from the region around the Baltic Sea, in northern Europe, and these have even survived winters in zone 3 when grown in a sheltered location and given a good protection of leaves for the winter.

Ivy has a rich history and has frequently been associated with holly. Both are much praised in old lore and Christmas hymns. The black berries were often associated with sin or darkness, while the red berries of the holly were associated with the blood of Christ. One is meant to cancel out the other. It was also highly revered by the druids and sometimes used for medicine. Poets were often crowned with ivy.

Everywhere I went in Galicia, ivy was creeping hither and yon. I particularly loved to see it snaking its way into crumbling stone buildings and climbing up the steeples of churches. To see ivy, so sacred to the druids, deftly picking its way over Christendom's most revered buildings gave me a guilty little thrill. I wondered how many knew of ivy's pre-Christian past and whether it would still be tolerated scampering over their church roofs and reaching up to their bells if they knew how it had been adored by pagans.

Everything humankind builds eventually crumbles. Our homes and our churches and our great castles and our bridges eventually return to dust. I find enormous comfort in the fact that nothing lasts forever. Great empires rise and inevitably fall. People came before us, and they will come after. Our lives are brief. I am here only for a short time. If I imagine myself as a house, I know that, one day, water will get in and my roof will leak and the walls will start to collapse. Floors will buckle and windows will break and maybe barn swallows will begin coming inside to nest. That would be nice. Eventually, the house will fall and the earth will gently and lovingly reclaim the wood and the nails and the stone. Ivy will grow over the foundation like a beautiful green blanket, and the place where the house once stood will be forgotten.

A LESS NATURAL form of decay, and a far less beautiful one, was the graffiti and vandalism we saw along the trail. The amount of it amazed me. The government had gone to some trouble to restore and replace crumbling and ruined waymarkers and make them visible and nice-looking. Most of them had originally had a small tab indicating the remaining distance to Santiago, but many of these had been removed. There were invariably meaningless sentiments written in every language where the numbers had been. Some days it was like being in a greeting card store, only more annoying. Things like "Live, Laugh, Love" and "Life Is Good" and "You Are Beautiful" were commonplace. I don't know why I found this so annoying, but I did.

On the entire trip, I saw only two phrases that actually had any meaning for me (and there was a *lot* of spray-painted messages on signs, underpasses, and so on). One of them was "The owl and the mouse cannot be friends and it is no one's fault," and the other was "Love is a rebel bird." Glenn and Sue, the couple from Texas we often walked with, also noticed the one about the rebel bird, and we talked about it later. (Sue was having issues with her foot and they often went slower than the rest of us, but we always caught up at the end of the day.) I told Glenn I was sure it must be a lyric from a song, but no one was sure which song. I later found out that it is a translation from one of the most famous arias in Georges Bizet's 1875 opera, *Carmen*. I liked it, and it seemed nice for the Camino. I liked it because it sounded mysterious, I love birds, and it sounds both nonsensical and logical at the same time. You can read into it what you wish and ascribe a lot of meaning to it or none. The Camino itself is kind of like that.

Wednesday, October 25–Thursday, October 26
Fonfría → San Mamede → Marcadoiro

THE PATH FROM Fonfría to San Mamede was as vibrant with gardens as the previous day's path had been. I was surprised to see bottlebrush trees (*Callistemon*) in flower, and they were alive with honeybees. Dahlias, hebes, mums, and asters were in abundance. I saw red carnations again, and many apple trees hung with fruit that was for some reason unpicked. Galicia must get reasonably cold in winter, because I passed some very large mock oranges, forsythia, roses, and lilacs, as well as a rosemary with the thickest branches I have ever seen. Large bowers of kiwifruit showed up in quite a number of places, many of them heavy with fruit, though it was hard and unripe. I saw a great many wagtails in Galicia, and this chipper little black and white bird does indeed wag its tail. I never stopped finding them charming.

I KNEW WE were nearing the end of the journey when, after leaving San Mamede, we passed through Sarria. From Sarria to Santiago is only one hundred kilometres, and many people choose to do just the last hundred kilometres of the Camino. From San Mamede to Marcadoiro it's mostly farm towns smelling of silage, with some oak and bracken fern forests in between. This is very peaceful, rather quiet country to walk in, and of course by the time you get to the last hundred kilometres, you've stopped thinking about how far you have to walk that day. By this point, the body has entirely adjusted, and you are free to simply enjoy yourself.

I was surprised by the plant life in Sarria, which was a weird blend of tender and tough. A few foxgloves were still in flower here and there, and cabbage palms and eucalyptus and camellias appeared. There was also oleander in abundance, and I even saw a fairly large banana tree. I realize now it must have been the Japanese banana (*Musa basjoo*), which can handle a bit of cold and frost in the winter. Acanthus, New Zealand flax, agapanthus, and a shrubby viburnum with a few pink flowers were fairly common sightings.

There were so many villages full of farm animals that the smell of sheep, cattle, and pigs was unmistakeable. In every single town, every single morning, I would hear one or more roosters crowing. I love that sound, as it takes me back to my childhood. Early on in the journey, I decided to give the rooster a name—Miguel (a good Spanish name)—and pretended that it was the same rooster crowing in every town and that he was doing the Camino with me. Every morning, when I heard him crowing, I imagined Miguel had left his albergue and that together we were heading down the path. One morning, as we heard the crowing even before dawn, I said to Isobel, "Miguel is rather ambitious, getting up before daylight today, isn't he?" and Isobel said, "Miguel?" I explained to her that the rooster was my Camino friend. Isobel said, "You can't just give him a name without giving him a backstory as well," so I did that too. I decided that his name was Miguel Sanchez, and that he was hatched in Majorca. His father had gone into the stewing pot when Miguel was still just a chick, and his devout mother grieved for her mate the rest of her days. She had always wanted to do the Camino, and especially to see the sacred chickens in Santo Domingo, but with all her egg laying and brooding, she had just never had the time or opportunity. Before settling down to a life of his own, Miguel decided to do the Camino in honour of his mother. When I told Isobel this, she gave me a funny look and said that I spent way too much time inside my own head.

Friday, October 27
Marcadoiro → Eirexe

WE STARTED OUT for Eirexe before dawn and walked through the most beautiful curtains of fog and mist as the sun was coming up. It was ethereal and unexpected. There were many gardens on this section of the path, and I marvelled at all the plants that were obviously there for no other reason than to be beautiful: palms, hydrangeas, lots of ivy, *Escallonia*, eucalyptus, fuchsias, laurel, yuccas, box, pampas grass. I saw a large fir tree in one corner, and there were old walls of stone that were beginning to crumble and cover themselves with moss. It was what I imagine Ireland looks like, and not really what I had expected from Spain.

I've always liked moss. I like how it looks; I like how it feels. I like finding it in unexpected places. I love all the various shades of green it comes in. I love how moss is not a respecter of persons or property; it will grow on the walls of castles and churches as easily as it does on a humble cabin in the woods. I can go anywhere on the planet and find mosses, and I certainly found it in Spain, often in the woods or growing along the walls of old buildings. "Hello, moss," I would silently greet this little carpet, and between us—I the "higher" life form and moss the "primitive"—I feel we had an understanding.

Where did life originate? Some will tell you that God created the heavens and the earth, as it says in the book of Genesis, and some will say that life evolved slowly over millions of years, and some of us, including me, don't really know. I don't much care, either. I wasn't there when it happened. A moss is no less miraculous because of how it got here. What matters is that it is here, and I love it, and I can find it anywhere. It is a consistent and elegant little friend. Like the Camino itself, moss is very simple, but that does not mean it is easy. It has a lot going on. For a plant that doesn't even have vascular tissue, it's very busy doing stuff like absorbing moisture or making spores or slowly spreading into those luxurious emerald carpets that I so cherish.

Everywhere we walked, when I looked for it, I found moss. The moss was doing what it has always done, which is mostly working on creating more moss. The tininess of this plant is a great advantage, as it allows mosses to inhabit nearly every corner of the earth. Evidently, one need not be large in order to be successful: there are more than twenty thousand species of moss. Moss finds for itself microecosystems where it can set about its work. It can grow on the branches of a tree or the roof of a building or even in cracks in a driveway. Most plants do not have such capabilities. The downside of being small is that if so much else is larger than you, you're going to constantly be in shadow, and plants need sunlight to flourish. Mosses have solved this problem by producing different chlorophyll than normal plants do. In the darkest corners and crevices of the forest, moss asserts itself, gently but insistently, begging you to caress it. I am always touching moss. I have to stroke it with my fingertips; I have to marvel at it. Why so luminous in such dark places, little moss friend?

Mosses live in a fascinating place called the boundary layer. This is that narrow zone where earth and atmosphere meet, and so mosses spread out and become deeply intimate with whatever space they have chosen. Watch how gently mosses creep over a rock, softening its lines, and how tenderly they brush the earth with their small green hands. The boundary layer actually traps heat and carbon dioxide and water vapour as well. Mosses make good use of these resources. They can only grow if it is moist, and when it is not, photosynthesis and growth must cease. Mosses do not mind. They are patient. They grow slowly, but they are long-lived. They do not hurry.

Saturday, October 28
Eirexe → Melide

BY NOW WE were only a few days from Santiago, and the walks were particularly beautiful. Again, we left before sunrise, and in the beam of Carol's headlamp, I saw a smallish animal go scurrying by. "Carol!" I said. "What's that over there?" She managed to get her light on it, and to my surprise and great joy it was a little hedgehog. Upon being discovered, it pulled its face down underneath itself and raised up its spines to be as prickly and formidable as possible. I was very pleased to make its acquaintance. European hedgehogs (larger than the kind kept as pets) feature in a lot of European children's stories, and they are wonderful little creatures. One of my favourite novels *ever* is *The Elegance of the Hedgehog* by French author Muriel Barbery. A young woman describes an older woman she knows (who is central to the plot) as rather like a hedgehog—very prickly and antisocial, yet with a certain unexpected elegance. Hedgehogs are nocturnal, mind their own business, and are excellent foragers. When threatened, they roll up into an impenetrable prickly ball, which is the most glorious defense system ever. I wish I could do that. Imagine being in a meeting somewhere, or having a fight with your sweetheart, and being able to just roll up into a prickly ball when you didn't like how things were unfolding. You could make yourself unavailable for a while without leaving the room and no one could get you. Brilliant. "Well, there's no point in trying to reason with Lyndon now," they would say. "He's rolled himself up into a ball again and can't be persuaded to talk. I guess we'll just have to wait until he calms down!" In 2015, British environment minister Rory Stewart gave an impassioned fifteen-minute speech about hedgehogs in the House of Commons, and it was one of the greatest events in the history of Britain's parliament. Several newspapers said it was absolutely the best speech of the year. They were not wrong. I hadn't expected to see a hedgehog on our journey (our wildlife sightings were very few), but it was certainly thrilling when it happened.

We had a good day of walking after that through pine and oak forest, past gardens with autumn sage (*Salvia greggii*) in flower and even some very large flowering maples (*Abutilon*). *Arum italicum* grew in a few of the shady, moist places. I was looking forward to being in Melide, a small city that is known throughout Spain for serving particularly delicious octopus, called *pulpo* by the Spanish. I was also running out of cash and really needed to find an ATM. When we got to Melide, we checked into our albergue, and then we decided to go out and look around a bit. Sue stayed behind because her leg was bothering her, but Carol, Mark, Isobel, Glenn, and I decided we would go see what the town was all about. I found an ATM in the front lobby of a closed bank, and my companions waited for me outside.

I inserted my card into the machine, and it helpfully asked me what language I would like service in. I chose English. It then asked me what I would like to do, and I said that I would like to withdraw €250, more than adequate funds to last the rest of my trip. This was also pretty much all I had left in that account, because I had budgeted for this journey very carefully and responsibly. The ATM began whirring and asked if I would like a receipt. I said that yes, I would. "Please take your cash," said the machine. Umm . . . there was no cash coming out. I poked the little silver slot where the money was supposed to emerge and nothing happened. The receipt printed. "Thank you for your transaction," said the machine. I stood there for a moment, dumbfounded. The ATM *said* that it had just given me cash, but it didn't actually *give* me any cash. I stared at the receipt incredulously. It said that I had just made a withdrawal. It thanked me for my withdrawal. The only problem was that a withdrawal did not actually occur.

My companions were sitting on a little bench just a short distance away, so I stuck my head out the door. "Isobel, could you come here for a second?" She walked over. "Yes?" As calmly as I could, I explained, "Uh, the machine says it gave me cash, but it, um, it didn't actually give me any cash." "Uh-oh," said Isobel.

This was late on a Saturday afternoon, which is why the bank was closed. The next day, the bank would still be closed, and on Monday we would be walking heaven knows where, and Tuesday we were due to arrive in Santiago. I fought panic. What on earth was I going to do? I explained to the others what had just happened. They were as shocked as I was. Carol, very sensibly, said, "We need to call your bank." I agreed that was a good idea.

We found a nice little corner café, I got out my debit card, and, using Carol's cell phone, I dialled the number on the back of the card. I reached someone in Canada and explained the situation to him. He seemed concerned but was nowhere near the level of concerned that I was. I was trying really hard not to freak out at this point, and that was when Isobel told me I was doing a really good job of not freaking out. That almost made me lose my composure on the spot. My bank said that they would have to "conduct an investigation" and proceeded to issue me an investigation number. I was told to keep the ATM receipt. The man on the phone said, "You'll most likely be refunded, but it can take up to sixty business days. I would recommend that you also speak to the Spanish bank whose ATM you used." The transaction, he said, had indeed gone through. I thanked him and got off the phone.

That amount of euros worked out to $384 Canadian, not a negligible amount of money for me. What, pray tell, was I supposed to do in the meantime with no money to speak of? I had exactly twenty-five euros in my pocket at that moment. I said to my fellow travellers, "You guys? I *really* need a drink." We found a bar, and our waiter brought us the largest sangrias I had ever seen in my life, and while I'm not an advocate for letting alcohol solve your problems, in this instance it made a world of difference. I think, after a single one of those *monstro* sangrias, I may have actually been a bit drunk. We went back to our albergue and told Sue what had happened. I said, quite honestly, "I have no idea what I'm going to do about this."

While I was pondering my predicament, Isobel said, "We've solved your issue," and handed me €250. "This is from Mark and me, and Glenn and Sue, and Carol. You're with friends. You don't need to worry. You don't need to pay any of us back. Just enjoy the rest of your Camino. We've got this."

I was so astonished I don't even remember what I said. I hope it was something along the lines of "thank you," but stronger and with great feeling. I was floored by this act of great generosity and really didn't know how to respond. There is an expression quoted often by those who walk this pilgrimage, and that is "the Camino provides." I have to say, it really does, and I was (and am) so grateful that this group of kind people took such good care of me. I am really not sure what I would have done without them. That evening, we went out (once the sangrias wore off, seriously) and we did try the octopus. It was the best I've ever had.

LATER, WHEN WE got to Santiago, I would find a branch of the bank whose ATM I used and I went in with Glenn, who spoke some Spanish. He explained the situation to one of the staff, and we waited while a series of phone calls was made. After about forty minutes, one of the bank staff who spoke some English came over to me. She told me that I would be refunded but that it would take five to ten days. She gave me her business card. I thanked her profusely, and we left. More than a month after I arrived home, a refund quietly showed up in my account.

Sunday, October 29
Melide → Salceda

ON THE WAY to Salceda, we came upon gorgeous forests of eucalyptus. They reminded me, of course, of when I lived in Australia in my early twenties. All the eucalyptus was planted—for timber, I imagine—and the sound of the wind in their canopies and their scent and the abundant bark and leaf litter beneath them was so uncannily like being back in Australia that I all but forgot I was in Spain.

Eucalypts are almost endlessly fascinating. These are old plants that are well represented in the fossil record and date back to at least twenty million years ago. They are cultivated in every country in the world where they are able to grow, but they are mostly native to Australia. (A few species are found in Papua New Guinea and Indonesia, and one species reaches as far north as the Philippines.) They are valued for their highly antibacterial oil, their timber, their beauty, the honey produced from their flowers, the wonderful dappled shade they provide, and their ability to grow rapidly under often adverse conditions. The leaves can also be used to create some extraordinarily beautiful dyes. Some of them have become invasive outside of their homeland, but for the most part they are highly regarded. These are also the only trees in the world that koalas can feed on, and there are only about fourteen or so species that they find suitable.

All of the eucalypts are evergreen, but they shed a lot of leaves rich in oils that are both antibacterial and antifungal. This means that a lot of litter develops beneath these trees, because it is extremely difficult for microorganisms to break them down and start the decomposition process. On warm days, eucalypt forests create a blue, smog-like haze as these oils evaporate. This creates the blue glow that gives Australia's Blue Mountains their name.

Eucalypts are superbly adapted to dealing with heat and drought. They will turn their leaves, which are usually long and narrow, to orient them in such a way as to diffuse the harshest rays of the sun. Leaves are always strongly fragrant when broken or crushed, and it is very common for eucalypts to have quite different foliage in their juvenile stage than they do when they are mature. The bark of these trees is highly variable and often exfoliating. Many eucalypts drop seemingly endless quantities of bark, either in long strips or in large, patchy flakes. They develop quite a mess beneath them, and eucalypt forests are very quick to go up in flames as a result of not only the highly flammable oils they produce but also the abundant litter beneath them. In many cases, the bark is extremely beautiful and quite diverse. In addition to being a potential fire hazard, in times of extreme drought eucalypts are known to simply drop large branches with no apparent warning. This is a means of reducing water usage but can lead to smashed cars and occasionally human deaths, especially while camping. Some gum trees, as they are known in their homeland, are more prone to this than others.

Eucalypt flowers are often small and not particularly showy, with most being either white or cream in colour. There are some bold exceptions to this, however, and some species have extravagantly beautiful flowers, which can be yellow, red, or pink, as well as white. Petals would be quick to dehydrate in the landscapes that eucalypts favour, so they simply don't produce any; they are a strictly "stamens only" kind of plants. Honey made from eucalyptus is often strongly flavoured, and some kinds of eucalyptus are said to produce the finest honey in the world.

I'm not sure what species of eucalyptus I saw in Spain, but there was a marked difference in the foliage between the juvenile trees and the adults. Some of them were absolutely enormous, and the distinctive silver-blue colouring of their leaves made them very visible even from a long distance away. In the last days of the journey there were quite a lot of them.

Monday, October 30
Salceda → Lavacolla

LEAVING SALCEDA WAS the first and only time on the journey I saw persimmon trees. They were in fruit and very beautiful. And when we reached Lavacolla, apart from finding the usual array of walking stick cabbages and bracken fern, I encountered another unexpected plant: the tea tree.

Tea tree (*Leptospermum*) is the name given to a group of evergreen, very twiggy shrubs or small trees mostly from the southern hemisphere. (They should not be confused with the related genus *Melaleuca*, which is also called tea tree.) About eighty species are known and most of them are Australian. There are two Asian species, and one that is found in both Australia and New Zealand. These plants have small, aromatic leaves that were historically used as a tea substitute and also for a variety of medicinal purposes. Flowers are often very beautiful, with five petals, which may be white, red, or pink. The ones I saw were flowering a little and they were vivid pink. They are very highly prized as bee forage and make exceedingly high-quality honey. Oils from these plants are also exceptionally antibacterial.

Leptospermum scoparium is by far the best-known species and is popular in gardens in both Australia and New Zealand. I've also seen it in California, but I did not know that it would be known to gardeners in Spain. Growing seven to fifteen feet tall, it produces small, scented leaves and beautiful, long-lasting sprays of white, or occasionally light pink, flowers. Many cultivars and hybrids have been developed, including several that have received the RHS award of merit. In New Zealand, it is known as manuka, where it is not only a prized honey and garden plant but also important in Maori culture.

Tuesday, October 31
Lavacolla → Santiago de Compostela

ON OCTOBER 31, after six weeks of walking, we made it to Santiago de Compostela. I didn't know what to think or how to feel, except that I was relieved it was over and that we had successfully done it. We'd had beautiful weather for the entire last ten days of our journey, but once we arrived in Santiago, rain started gently falling. It seemed fitting somehow.

We followed the trail of scallop shells into town and arrived at the cathedral. It was undergoing some repair and reconstruction, which still continues. All dressed in nets and scaffolding, it wasn't exactly the most picturesque cathedral we saw, but it was nevertheless very exciting to finally arrive. A man was playing bagpipes as we came into town, and we celebrated with sangrias and it was very nice. Large white camellias were beginning to flower, and I admired them as we made our way to the pilgrim's office. We presented our pilgrim's passports, which have to be stamped all along your journey as proof of where you've been, and they in turn presented us with beautiful certificates that declared, in Latin, our achievement of having walked eight hundred kilometres. "Congratulations," the woman at the desk said to me, and she seemed sincere.

The following day, All Saints Day, is a big deal in Spain. We went to the pilgrims' mass at the cathedral, which was significant in part because of the use of the *botafumeiro*. (I could never remember the name of this device and kept calling it the "swingie thing.") The *botafumeiro* is an enormous censer with incense smouldering inside. It is suspended on long ropes, and on important occasions it is swung through the nave of the cathedral trailing a cloud of incense, not only to purify the building and those present but also, originally, to cover up the stench of the road-weary pilgrims, who did not have the luxury of daily baths. It was a rather grand spectacle, and one that they don't put on every day.

STANDING IN THE Cathedral of Santiago de Compostela felt timeless and dreamlike at the same time. I could now count myself among the thousands who had made the journey successfully, and I pondered the lives of those who had not. I wondered how many devout people would have liked to stand in my shoes and hadn't been able to, so I tried to be especially respectful. There is a pillar as you enter that has been touched by pilgrims for centuries; you can clearly see the wear from thousands of hands over so much time, touching and touching the stone, over and over. I put my hand there too, as it seemed like the right thing to do.

There is an enormous, jewel-encrusted statue of St. James (which you are allowed to touch), and somewhat beneath that is the tomb where the saint rests. You can stand in line and pass beside his remains, but you can't touch the tomb because it is protected by a metal gate. (I actually had to stand in line twice. I didn't realize why we were standing in line and missed it the first time: I was looking straight ahead when I should have been looking to my left.) At the bars of the gate, people stop to say a brief prayer before moving on so the next pilgrim can have their turn. People put their hands through the gate and toss in papers with prayers written on them. The ground was covered with neatly folded papers. I wondered if these were cleaned up from time to time to make room for new papers. Surely the little room could not hold all the prayers that people leave behind. When I stood before the tomb of St. James, I felt a little undercurrent of something run through my soul. I'm not sure what it was. Excitement, perhaps. Gratitude, surely. I still wonder if he is really buried there, or if it's just a story.

I was looking in and wondering about this when I heard a sniffle and realized the pilgrim behind me was crying. It was a young woman I had seen on the trail a few times but had never talked to. I turned to her and she unexpectedly reached out and squeezed my hand. "Are you all right?" I asked her. "I am now," she said.

AFTERWORD

Some people walk the Camino many times in their lives, but I would not have an interest in doing it again. I am pleased, however, that I did it. I walked over hills and mountains. I walked through vineyards and farmland. I walked through charming little towns that have been there since the Middle Ages. I laughed and I was amused and I was irritated and annoyed. My feet and shoes did not disappoint me. They did what I asked of them. I ate some fabulous food in Spain, and some food that was bland and uninteresting. I got really sick of bread and vowed I would never eat it again. I ate fresh figs, fresh grapes, and fresh pears. I had really delicious tomatoes. Spain had so many flowers and trees, I never wanted for something to look at or admire. I saw rosemary and lavender in the wild while the most adorable lizards played on the warm slopes around them. The light was gorgeous. It was so interesting to walk along a path that has been walked for nearly two thousand years. The contours and colours of the land were robust and vivid; the dust on my shoes was like a benediction. I loved the way the sunlight curled around the endless stones at dawn and made me feel curious and engaged. I liked hearing Miguel crow every morning, and I liked the simplicity of what I did every day.

I don't know that one necessarily needs to think profound thoughts while on a pilgrimage. Maybe just doing one is enough. The ruins of monasteries and convents spoke to me, and I loved when the crumbling walls were reclaimed by ivies and grasses, which they often were. I sat under the shade of almond trees and marvelled at the land that has been walked over again and again, and again and again. It's possible that the Camino wasn't about me, and maybe had nothing to do with me. Perhaps I needed to be there so that one day my nephews would be inspired, or perhaps this small memoir might serve as a different kind of interpretation or guidepost for some. It's possible that life just happens sometimes, and that not everything has to mean something. If you are thinking about the world and your place in it, perhaps walking the Camino might help you sort that out. Perhaps when you stand under the field of stars, it will provide you with some clarity, or some understanding you didn't previously have. Wherever the path takes you, I hope the trees and flowers will bless you on your journey as they did me on mine.

ACKNOWLEDGEMENTS

A book doesn't happen by itself. It might be my name on the cover, but there's an entire team of very talented folks who worked behind the scenes to put it all together. I'm so grateful for all of you. I'd like to thank the staff at the University of Regina Press who worked so tirelessly on my behalf and wanted to hear this story, especially Bruce Walsh and Sean Prpick. My editor, Alex Schultz, deserves special recognition.

My family and friends have been very supportive of the work that I do in the world and were very gracious to me while I was writing. Kevin MacLean checked in regularly to make sure I hadn't died alone in my house, and Kate Kraft provided much-needed insight and wisdom. Mim Martin provided inspiration without even being aware that she was doing so. The rest of you (and you know who you are) should know how deeply thankful I am for you. I would also like to extend a special thank you to Michelle Day, along with the staff of and visitors to the Nikka Yuko Japanese Garden in Lethbridge.

I would be remiss if I did not express my gratitude to the other pilgrims I met along the trail and in particular Sandy, Glenn, Sue, Mark, and Isobel. I would like to thank the entire country of Spain for opening its borders and allowing thousands of strangers from all over the world to tramp across that beautiful land. What an extraordinary privilege. And thanks also to St. James himself and all the invisible powers at work in the universe that conspired to make the Camino de Santiago a possibility. It has done so much for so many.

Finally, I have to thank Carol Huber for her generosity and friendship. Her companionship and indomitable kingbird spirit along the trail pushed me and motivated me. She praised me, scolded me, and endured countless botanical observations over many long miles. She did this with a smile on her face and always looked for the positive in everything. I have to thank Carol's husband, Dan McKinnon, for allowing me to run off to Europe with his wife for six weeks, something a lesser man perhaps might have been less inclined to encourage. I also want to thank you, dear reader, for picking up this book and coming along with me on this journey.

PLANTS *of the* CAMINO DE SANTIAGO

PLANTS ARE LISTED by their common name where one exists, followed by their scientific name in italics. The scientific name, used consistently the world over, will specify exactly which genus and species is being referenced. Sometimes even the variety is mentioned. For example, the specific bird cherry mentioned on page 98 is *Prunus padus* var. *commutata*. Images are indicated with **bold** page numbers.

Acanthus — Stately perennials that comprise their own family, loved since Roman times. (123)

Agapanthus — South African perennials with strappy foliage and lily-like blooms, now grown all over the world. (123)

Agave — Sculptural, spiky plants mostly from Mexico and the American southwest. (18)

agrimony (*Agrimonia*) — A perennial in the rose family with a long history of medicinal use. (80)

alder (*Alnus*) — Smooth-barked trees closely related to birch. (80, 117)

alfalfa (*Medicago sativa*) — A worldwide crop used to make hay. (33)

Allium — The Latin name for onion, some of which are used in gardens as ornamentals. (38)

almond (*Prunus dulcis*) — Small tree prized

for its edible nuts and oil. (**29**, 30, 112, 138)

Aloe — A genus of succulent and often ornamental plants. (80)

alpine thistle (*Carlina acaulis*) — Famous rock garden perennial native to the Pyrenees. (12, **13**)

Angelica sylvestris — Plants in the carrot family with a long history of medicinal use. (94)

angel's trumpet (*Datura*) — Plants in the nightshade family grown for their fragrance and beautiful, trumpet-shaped flowers. A weed in many parts of the world; also a hallucinogen. (19, 62)

apple (*Malus*) — One of the most iconic fruits in the world and the tree that produces it. (122)

artichoke (*Cynara*) — A vegetable in the daisy family whose flowers buds are considered a delicacy. (38)

arum (*Arum italicum*) — A lovely perennial with arrow-shaped, silver-marked leaves and clusters of showy red berries. (127)

ash (*Fraxinus excelsior*) — Common shade tree. (15, 18, 34, 38, 54)

Asparagus — A prized vegetable since ancient times. New spring growth is the part that is eaten. (33)

Aster — Plants in the daisy family that often flower late in the year. (122)

bacopa (*Sutera cordata*) — A South African plant now widely used for baskets and containers. (93)

bamboo — Much-loved garden plants around the world, bamboos are grasses but unusual in that a great many of them form woody tissue. There are nearly 1,500 species in well over 100 different genera. (116)

barberry (*Berberis*) — Prickly shrubs that may be evergreen or deciduous and often have beautiful flowers or berries or both. (41)

beech (*Fagus*) — Gorgeous shade tree. (56, 57)

birch (*Betula*) — Shade trees with beautiful, slender twigs and often beautiful bark. (87, 98, 112, 115, 117)

bird cherry (*Prunus padus* var. *commutata*) — A cherry grown for its flowers rather than its fruit. We call it mayday in North America. (98)

blackberry (*Rubus*) — A very thorny relative of the raspberries. (72)

blackthorn (*Prunus spinosa*) — Also called sloe, this is a species of plum with smallish fruits that grows wild in much of Europe. (41)

bottlebrush (*Callistemon*) — An Australian genus in the myrtle family with unusual flowers shaped like bottlebrushes. (122)

box honeysuckle (*Lonicera nitida*) — A distinct species, box honeysuckle is so named because it resembles and is used like boxwood (*Bruxus*), a small evergreen shrub often used for hedges. (107)

bracken fern (*Pteridium aquilinum*) — One of the world's most widespread plants, a tall fern that often grows as an understory plant in large colonies. (98, 122, 132)

broom — Shrubs in either the genus *Genista* or *Cytisus*. They usually have yellow flowers. (117)

cabbage palm (*Cordyline australis*) — A palm-like tree native to New Zealand but now widely grown in mild, temperate places. (123)

Calendula — A common annual with bright orange or yellow daisy-like flowers. (62)

calla (*Zantedeschia*) — A popular plant with tubular, often white flowers. Frequently used by florists. (93, 112)

Calystegia — A type of morning glory with usually white blooms and often a weedy growth habit. (32)

Camellia — Evergreen, usually winter-flowering shrub. Very beautiful. (32, 123, 135)

cardoon (*Cynara*) — Very similar to artichoke. (38)

carnation (*Dianthus caryophyllus*) — A fragrant, much-loved flower around the world. The red carnation is Spain's national flower. (45, 73, 122)

Catalpa — Magnificent shade tree with large leaves and white flowers. (87)

cauliflower (*Brassica oleracea*) — A plant in the cabbage family whose flower buds are eaten. (62)

cedar (*Cedrus*) — Refers to *Cedrus*, the true cedars. The plants we call cedar in North America are *Thuja*. Both are dense evergreens much used in cities and gardens. (51)

cedar of Lebanon (*Cedrus libani*) — A true species of cedar prized for centuries for its timber and beauty. (87)

celandine (*Chelidonium majus*) — A weedy plant in the poppy family with a long history of medicinal use. (31)

Centaurea calcitrapa — Often called cornflowers. Perennials and weeds in the daisy family. (94)

chestnut (*Castanea*) — A large, beautiful tree with edible nuts. (xviii, 56, 99, 100, 102, 105, 115–17)

chicory (*Cichorium intybus*) — Daisy family plant with blue flowers. (19, **20**, 21)

Chinese fan palm (*Trachycarpus*) — One of the hardiest palms in the world, often grown as a street tree. (106)

Chrysanthemum — Perennial in the daisy family with single or double flowers. Often affectionately called "mums." (117)

crepe myrtle (*Lagerstroemia indica*) — A beautiful flowering tree from Asia, but not a true species of myrtle. (32)

Crocus — Very beautiful flowers in the iris family. (12–13, 32)

Cupid's dart (*Catananche caerulea*) — Daisy family plant with blue-purple or white flowers. Once used for love potions. (32)

cypress, Leyland cypress (*Cupressus* x *leylandii*) — One of the most widely grown evergreen conifers in the world. (32, 83)

Dahlia — A plant in the daisy family with very showy flowers in many colours. (91, 93, 122)

Darwin's barberry (*Berberis darwinii*) — A spiny, small evergreen shrub with attractive fruits and flowers. Named to honour Charles Darwin. (90)

Douglas fir (*Pseudotsuga menziesii*) — North American conifer much planted for timber in other parts of the world. (72)

Echium vulgare — Also called Viper's bugloss. A plant in the borage family once grown for medicinal use. (33)

edible fig (*Ficus carica*) — Figs comprise their own family. Common fig, edible fig, and fig are usually references to *Ficus carica*. Edible fig is a proper name for this species. If you've eaten a fig before, it's this one. (7, 18, 23–24, **25**, 26–27, 38, 54, 93, 137) elder (*Sambucus*) — Large shrub with dense clusters of berries. (31, 98)

Escallonia — A pretty shrub with attractive leaves and flowers. (124)

Eucalyptus — Large Australian trees now grown in many parts of the world. (72, 106, 123, 124, 130–32)

evening primrose (*Oenothera*) — A common weed or wildflower with large flowers that are usually yellow and usually open in the evening. (54, 116)

fennel (*Foeniculum vulgare*) — A common plant with a feathery shape and closely related to dill. Often used for food and medicine. (31)

fig (*see* edible fig)

fir (*Abies*) — A large conifer. (124)

flowering maple (*Abutilon*) — A member of the mallow family so named because of its maple-like foliage. (55, 127)

Forsythia — A spring-flowering shrub in the olive family. (34, 122)

four o'clock (*Mirabilis jalapa*) — A South American plant with showy, tubular flowers that open late in the afternoon, hence the common name. (18, 32, 54)

foxglove (*Digitalis purpurea*) — A common perennial with tall spires of (usually) purple or pink flowers. (123)

Fuchsia — A common flower often grown in hanging baskets and containers. (124)

Gaillardia — Sometimes called blanket flower, a North American species of daisy widely cultivated as an ornamental. (93)

garlic (*Allium sativum*) — An onion-like plant whose bulb is used for food and flavouring. (111)

geranium (*Pelargonium*) — South African flower popular in gardens around the world. (15, 80)

gladioli (*Gladiolus*) — Common garden plant often used by florists. (91, 95)

globe thistle (*Echinops*) — A large perennial so named because of the spherical shape of the buds and flowers. (33)

gorse (*Ulex*) — A shrubby, very prickly plant in the bean family that has become a weed in many parts of the world. (117)

grape (*Vitis*) — Refers to both the fruit and the vine it grows on. (18, 33, 63–64, **65**, 66, 84, 137)

hawthorn (*Crataegus*) — A large shrub or small tree in the rose family, often with sharp spines and showy berries. (15, 98)

hazelnut (*Corylus*) — Commonly grown shrub with delicious, edible nuts. (15, 55)

heather — A common term for a group of usually evergreen shrubs and perennials in the blueberry family. They are either in the genus *Calluna* or *Erica* and are often autumn or winter flowering. (117)

Hebe — A genus of shrubby, attractive plants closely related to the perennial *Veronica*. (122)

hellebore (*Helleborus*) — A perennial in the buttercup family, usually evergreen and often winter blooming. (32)

hens and chicks (*Sempervivum*) — Common succulent perennials. (116)

herb of St. James (*Senecio*) — A tall plant in the daisy family with gorgeous yellow blooms, common along the Camino. (95)

holly (*Ilex*) — Large shrubs that may be evergreen or deciduous and famed for their showy berries. (112, 119) hollyhock (*Althea*) — A common garden flower that is usually very tall. (39, 112)

honey locust (*Gleditsia*) — A shade tree in the bean family with very lovely foliage and often planted along streets and boulevards. (53)

horse chestnut (*Aesculus hippocastanum*) — A common shade tree with large, inedible nuts. (18, 100, 102–4)

Hosta — A common perennial mostly grown for its attractive foliage. (18, 112)

Hydrangea — A common shrub with large clusters of showy flowers. (62, 112, 124)

impatiens (*Impatiens balfourii*) — Different than the impatiens we grow as bedding plants; this is a species with unusually shaped, usually pink blossoms. (18, 70, 112)

ivy (*Hedera helix*) — A very common European vine with evergreen foliage. (118–19, **120**, 121, 124)

ivy geranium (*Pelargonium peltatum*) — A type of popular, window-box geranium with ivy-like foliage and prized for its ease of care and long season of bloom. (18, 54, 70, **71**, 112)

Japanese banana (*Musa basjoo*) — An ornamental species of banana prized for its enormous and beautiful leaves, the Japanese banana is hardier and differs from the tropical bananas. (123)

Japanese creeper (*Parthenocissus*) — A large climbing plant in the grape family. (51)

kale (*Brassica oleracea*) — Common leafy vegetable not unlike cabbage. (95, 112)

kiwifruit (*Actinidia*) — The name for a smallish, delicious fruit and the vine it grows on. (122)

knapweed (*Centaurea spp.*) — Plants in the daisy family that can be pretty but are often roadside weeds. (94)

laurel (*Prunus laurocerasus*) — A common broadleaf evergreen, frequently used for hedges and windbreaks. (32, 124)

lavender (*Lavendula*) — A highly fragrant Mediterranean herb. (32, 80, 93, 137)

leek (*Allium ampeloprasum*) — An onion-like plant in which the elongated stem (rather than the bulb) is eaten. (80)

lemon balm (*Melissa officinalis*) — A plant in the mint family whose foliage smells strongly of lemon. Often used for food and medicine. (93)

lichen — A curious symbiotic relationship between blue-green algae and fungi. There are over 15,000 species found throughout the world. Lichens often grow on rocks and trees, and many of them are quite beautiful. (109)

licorice fern (*Polypodium glycyrrhiza*) — A common fern that grows as an epiphyte, with rhizomes that smell strongly of licorice when broken. (109)

lilac (*Syringa*) — Popular and very fragrant spring-flowering shrub. (12, 18, 34, 35, 122)

linden (*Tilia*) — A beautiful shade tree with highly fragrant blooms and nice fall colour. (52, 55, 87)

Lobelia — Common garden flower for pots and containers. (15)

locust (*Robinia*) — A gorgeous shade tree with beautiful spring flowers. (70)

London plane (*Platanus* x *acerifolia*) — One of the most popular shade/street trees in the world. (55, 76)

Magnolia — Spectacular flowering large shrub or tree. (87)

Malva — A genus of plants in the mallow family prized for their pink or purple flowers. (33)

marigold (*Tagetes*) — Common garden flower that is usually orange, yellow, or gold in colour. (15, 54, 112)

marsh mallow (*Althaea officinalis*) — Perennial in the mallow family and an ancient vegetable. (38, **39**, 40)

Mimulus — A garden plant with bright, tubular flowers. (70)

mint (*Mentha*) — A very fragrant perennial with a long history of culinary and medicinal use. (93)

mock orange (*Philadelphus*) — A gorgeous, hardy shrub with white flowers that both resemble and smell of orange blossoms, hence the name. (122)

monkey puzzle tree (*Araucaria araucana*) — A South American conifer with very sharp, spiny leaves and trunks. (90)

moss — Ancient, nonvascular plants that fill forests and moist places with that gorgeous, soft carpet of green. Mosses comprise their own family and there are around 12,000 species known worldwide. (105, 124–26)

mountain ash (*Sorbus*) — Trees in the rose family prized for their showy berries. Also called rowan. (59, 98)

mountain mallow (*Iliamna*) — Plants in the mallow family closely related to hollyhocks. (38–**39**)

musk mallow (*Malva moschata*) — A common garden perennial with soft pink flowers. (33, 40)

New Zealand flax (*Phormium*) — A very large perennial with long, strappy leaves. Looks somewhat like an enormous grass. (123)

oak (*Quercus*) — One of the most common trees in the world. (xviii, 13, 15, 32, 38, 54, 56–60, 98, **99**, 117, 122, 127)

oleander (*Nerium oleander*) — A beautiful shrub with lovely flowers and foliage; very poisonous if eaten. (15, 18, 52, **53**, 93, 123)

olive (*Olea europaea*) — The name of the fruit and the tree that bears it; olives are pressed for oil and preserved, but never eaten raw. (32, 33, 34–35, **36**, 37–38, 45)

orchid cactus (*Epiphyllum*) — A rainforest cactus commonly cultivated for its enormous, showy flowers. (116)

pampas grass (*Cortaderia*) — A huge grass from South America with showy, fluffy white plumes. (124)

passionflower (*Passiflora*) — A lovely flowering vine with beautiful flowers that yield passionfruit in some species. (38)

Paulownia — An incredible, large tree with beautiful, tubular purple flowers in spring. (53, 87)

peach (*Prunus persica*) — Delicious fruit and the tree that produces it. Usually golden or soft orange in colour. (30, 112–13)

pear (*Pyrus*) — Delicious fruit and the tree that produces it. Fruits range from yellow to red. (109, 137)

peony (*Paeonia*) — A much-loved perennial with enormous flowers. (18)

pepper (*Capsicum*) — The large fruits of a plant closely related to tomatoes and eggplants. (110, 116)

persimmon (*Diospyros kaki*) — A highly prized fruit that is usually orangey-red in colour. (132)

Petunia — One of the most common garden plants in the world. Frequently used for pots and containers. (15, 45, 54, 70, 112)

pincushion flower (*Scabiosa*) — A lovely perennial with fluffy, double flowers. (19)

pine (*Pinus*) — A very common evergreen tree. (18, 98, 115, 127)

plum (*Prunus*) — Delicious fruit and the tree that produces it. Fruits may be any number of colours but are usually red, purplish, or gold. (41)

poinsettia (*Euphorbia pulcherrima*) — Perennial often used as a Christmas decoration. (80)

poplar (*Populus*) — Very common shade tree all over the world. (33, 80)

poppy (*Papaver*) — Plants prized for their lovely blooms, medicinal properties, and edible seeds. (33)

prickly pear (*Opuntia*) — A type of cactus that is very ornamental and also sometimes grown as a barrier plant or for its spiny, edible fruits. (113)

pride of Barbados (*Caesalpinia pulcherrima*) — An incredibly beautiful, highly prized subtropical shrub. (90)

pumpkin (*Cucurbita pepo*) — Famous vegetable in the squash family. (40, 45, 46, 110)

Pyrenean oak (*Quercus pyrenaica*) — A slow-growing oak species from southwestern Europe and the northern parts of Africa. Common in many parts of Spain. (98, **99**)

Queensland palm (*Macrozamia moorei*) — A large cycad that masquerades as a palm and is often grown as a street tree. (52)

quince (*Cydonia oblonga*) — A name given to a tree

and its pear-like, edible fruit. (63, 109–10, **111**)

Rosa x 'Camino de Santiago' — A hybrid cultivar of rose developed in Logroño, Spain, especially to honour those walking the pilgrimage. (53)

rose (*Rosa*) — Prickly shrubs prized for centuries for their beauty and fragrance. (15, 18, 62, 70, 80, 83, 91, 122)

rosemary (*Rosmarinus*) — Strongly scented and flavoured Mediterranean shrub much used for cooking. (54, 80, **81**, 122, 137)

St. Mary's thistle, milk thistle (*Silybum marianum*) — A very prickly and pretty plant prized for its beauty and medicinal use. (54)

Salvia — The Latin name for all true species of sage. Very fragrant plants in the mint family, some grown for their beauty, some their scent, and some both. (32, 127)

Scotch pine (*Pinus sylvestris*) — Tree native to Eurasia and much planted for timber. (72, 117)

sea buckthorn (*Hippophae rhamnoides*) — A large, spiny shrub with stunning orange berries. (35)

sea holly (*Eryngium campestre*) — A prickly, thistle-like perennial that is often quite beautiful. (94)

Sedum — Well-known perennial with pretty flowers and very succulent foliage. (31, 109)

silk tree (*Albizia julibrissin*) — A large shrub in the bean family with feathery leaves and fluffy, gorgeous flowers. (53)

silver lace vine (*Polygonum aubertii*) — A common vine in the buckwheat family so named for its lacy, pretty white blooms that appear late in the year. (5, 32)

silver poplar (*Populus alba*) — A beautiful large tree

with white bark and silver, three-pointed leaves. It is often mistaken for a maple. (51)

sloe (*see* blackthorn)

snapdragon (*Antirrhinum*) — Common garden flower around the world. (31)

snow on the mountain (*Euphorbia marginata*) — A white and green species of spurge that is cultivated infrequently. (70)

southern magnolia (*Magnolia grandiflora*) — A large, striking distinct species of magnolia. (33)

Spanish chestnut (*Castanea sativa*) — A gorgeous, large tree with edible nuts. (**101**)

spurge (*Euphorbia*) — Mostly perennials grown for their unusual flowers. (33)

squash (*Cucurbita*) — A pretty delicious vegetable. (18, 45, 46)

sunflower (*Helianthus annuus*) — Common garden plant. (62)

sweet william (*Dianthus barbatus*) — An old-fashioned garden plant closely related to carnations. (80)

sycamore (*Acer pseudoplatanus*) — A common shade tree. (55)

teasel (*Dipsacus*) — A very tall perennial not unlike a thistle. (32)

tea tree (*Leptospermum*) — A group of shrubs prized for their beauty and fragrance. (132, **133**)

tomato (*Solanum lycopersicum*) — A delicious vegetable you are likely to have encountered before. (84, 95, 116, 137)

tree of heaven (*Ailanthus altissima*) — A beautiful Asian tree that has become a serious weed in many parts of the world. (87)

trumpet vine (*Campsis*) — A large, woody vine with trumpet-shaped, extremely beautiful large flowers. (51)

tulip tree (*Liriodendron*) — A very big tree with flowers that resemble tulip blossoms. Closely related to magnolias. (87)

Umbilicus — Kind of a weird plant with very round, succulent foliage. (109)

Viburnum — A genus of shrubs grown for both their flowers and berries. (123)

Virginia creeper (*Parthenocissus*) — A very large, smothering vine. (63)

walking stick cabbage (*Brassica oleracea* var. *longata*) — A peculiar vegetable that forms a tall stalk instead of a head like usual cabbages. (112, 117, 132)

walnut (*Juglans regia*) — An enormous and beautiful shade tree, prized for its edible nuts. (**8**, 9, 31, 54, 93)

willow (*Salix*) — Fast-growing, immense tree. (51, 55, 80, 87)

Wisteria — A long-lived vine in the bean family with stunning, long clusters of showy flowers. (108)

yew (*Taxus*) — A common evergreen shrub or tree that produces fleshy berries instead of the cones we usually expect from conifers. (15, 32, 59)

Yucca — A very spiky evergreen perennial with stunning spires of ivory-coloured blooms. (70, 124)

Zinnia — A brightly coloured, very common garden flower. (90, 93–94)

ILLUSTRATION CREDITS

PAGE 8: Walnut (*Juglans regia*). Köhler Walnuss 1887. Public Domain image / Wikimedia Commons.

PAGE 13: Alpine thistle (*Carlina acaulis*). Illustration Carlina acaulis. From Prof. Dr. Otto Wilhelm Thomé's *Flora von Deutschland, Österreich und der Schweiz* 1885, Gera, Germany. Public Domain image / Wikimedia Commons.

PAGE 20: Chicory (*Cichorium intybus*). Illustration Cichorium intybus. From Prof. Dr. Otto Wilhelm Thomé's *Flora von Deutschland, Österreich und der Schweiz* 1885, Gera, Germany. Public Domain image / Wikimedia Commons.

PAGE 25: Edible fig (*Ficus carica*). Ficus carica. Public Domain image / Wikimedia Commons.

PAGE 29: Almond (*Prunus dulci*). From Prof. Dr. Otto Wilhelm Thomé's *Flora von Deutschland, Österreich und der Schweiz* 1885, Gera, Germany. Public Domain image / Wikimedia Commons.

PAGE 36: Olive (*Olea europaea*). *Köhler's Medizinal-Pflanzen in naturgetreuen Abbildungen mit kurz erläuterndem Texte (Plate 109)*. Public Domain image / Wikimedia Commons.

PAGE 39: Marsh mallow (*Althaea officinalis*). *Köhler's Medizinal-Pflanzen in naturgetreuen Abbildungen mit kurz erläuterndem Texte* (Plate 42). Public Domain image / Wikimedia Commons.

PAGE 53: Oleander (*Nerium oleander*). Die Giftpflanzen Deutschlands (1910). Public Domain image / Wikimedia Commons.

PAGE 65: Grape (*Vitis vinifera*). From Prof. Dr. Otto Wilhelm Thomé's *Flora von Deutschland, Österreich und der Schweiz* 1885, Gera, Germany. Public Domain image. Wikimedia Commons.

PAGE 71: Ivy geranium (*Pelargonium peltatum*). *The Botanical Magazine*, Plate 20 (Volume 1, 1787). Public Domain image / Wikimedia Commons.

PAGE 81: Rosemary (*Rosmarinus*). From Prof. Dr. Otto Wilhelm Thomé's *Flora von Deutschland, Österreich und der Schweiz* 1885, Gera, Germany. Public Domain image / Wikimedia Commons.

PAGE 99: Pyrenean oak (*Quercus pyrenaica*). From *Traité des Arbres et Arbustes que l'on cultive en France en pleine terre* (1801–1819) by Pierre-Joseph Redouté. Original from the New York Public Library. Digitally enhanced by rawpixel. Public Domain image.

PAGE 101: Spanish chestnut (*Castanea sativa*). Prof. Dr. Otto Wilhelm Thomé's *Flora von Deutschland, Österreich und der Schweiz* 1885, Gera, Germany. Public Domain image / Wikimedia Commons.

PAGE 111: Quince (*Cydonia oblonga*). Cydonia oblonga. Public Domain image / Wikimedia Commons.

PAGE 120: Ivy (*Hedera helix*). From Prof. Dr. Otto Wilhelm Thomé's *Flora von Deutschland, Österreich und der Schweiz* 1885, Gera, Germany. Public Domain image / Wikimedia Commons.

PAGE 133: Tea tree (*Leptospermum scoparium*). Leptospermum scoparium nichollii. From Curtis's *Botanical Magazine*, London., vol. 138. Public Domain image / Wikimedia Commons.

PHOTO: TED DELLER

ABOUT THE AUTHOR

A gardener, environmentalist, and wanderer, LYNDON PENNER grew up in Saskatchewan and has loved the natural world his entire life. He is a gardening expert, a former columnist for the CBC, and the author of several books, including *Native Plants for the Short Season Yard*. Lyndon lives in Saskatoon, Saskatchewan.

A NOTE ABOUT THE TYPE

THE BODY OF this book is set in *Adobe Jenson Pro*. It is an old-style serif typeface that captures the essence of Nicolas Jenson's roman and Ludovico degli Arrighi's italic typeface designs. The combined strength and beauty of these two icons of Renaissance type result in an elegant typeface suited to a broad spectrum of applications. Designed by Robert Slimbach of the Adobe type design team, *Adobe Jenson Pro* is part of the family of Adobe Originals historical revivals, including *Adobe Garamond Pro* and *Adobe Caslon Pro*.